LIQUOR UP FRONT, POKER IN THE REAR

A BOOK OF ADULT HUMOR

By Mike Hunt

All Rights Reserved
ISBN 978-0-9817007-7-9
Copyright © 2011 by S&B Publishing

This book may not be reproduced in whole or in part without the written permission of the author or the publisher.

First Printing – January 2011
Printed in the United States of America

www.AllAmericanBooks.com

Liquor Up Front, Poker in the Rear

Liquor Up Front, Poker in the Rear

Disclaimer

The majority of the jokes contained in this book are based upon material which is freely available in the public domain. No information as to who wrote the original versions of these jokes was available to the author. If anyone has a valid claim to the copyright ownership of the root of any joke contained herein, please contact the publisher so that proper accreditation may be given in any future edition.

Liquor Up Front, Poker in the Rear

Liquor Up Front, Poker in the Rear

Laugh...

Because smiling is the second best thing you can do with your mouth!

Liquor Up Front, Poker in the Rear

Liquor Up Front, Poker in the Rear

TABLE OF CONTENTS

The Best Medicine 13
Voodoo Penis 17
Medical Condition 21
Side Effects 22
Did You Jump? 23
The Second Time 25
Flat Tummy 27
Little Soldier 28
Poker Player 29
Christmas Party 32
Cowboy Up 34
I Have A Plan 35
Always Tell the Truth 37
Family Resemblance 38
Private Parts 39
Common Courtesy 40
Tit For Tat 42
Final Confession 43
Night On the Town 44
Drop the Soap 46
Sex Frog 48
True Confession 50
No More For You! 52
Frozen Skunk 54
Moby Dick's Son 55
The Rich Hooker 57
Elder Sex 60

Liquor Up Front, Poker in the Rear

Sensitivity Test For Men 62
The Pickle Slicer 65
Ball Four 66
Little Blue Pill 67
Holy Hot Dogs 68
Two Brothers 69
Quick Thinking 71
Close Call 73
Texas Woman 75
Jack and Debra 76
The Toast 77
The Face Lift 79
Baby Texan 81
Sexual Harassment 83
Osama & the Genie 84
Firm Up 86
Newlyweds 87
Nag, Nag, Nag 89
All Aboard! 91
Basic Math 93
Medical Miracle 95
Harry 96
My First Time 99
Human Kindness 101
A Good Deal 102
Lady Golfer 105
Barbie Doll 109
Finished? 110
Sperm Count 112
The Peaches 114
The Dildo 116
Drug Research 117

Liquor Up Front, Poker in the Rear

Devil of a Deal 119
Happy Birthday 121
Cheap Diagnosis 123
Little Genie 126
A Fairy Tale 128
Amazing Claude 130
Happy Anniversary 132
It's The Thought 133
The Eulogy 134
Three Virgins 135
Jolt of Caffeine 137
Choo Choo! 139
Fill 'Er Up 141
Safe Smokes 143
Five Secrets to a Perfect Relationship 144
The Amazing Texan 145
Cathouse Parrot 147
Learning To Cuss 149
Miss Manners 151
Remember Me? 152
Teenage Sex 154
The "F" Word 155
Logical Deduction 157
Traffic Stop 159
Divorce Letter 160
Frank Feldman 165
Tee'd Off 167
Old Cowboy 170
The Fishing Trip 172
All That Glitters 173
Poison Pill 174
Jungle Sex 175

Liquor Up Front, Poker in the Rear

String Him Up!	176
A La Carte Menu	177
Speak!	179
Deaf Dog	181
Stowaway	182
Two Bags Full	184
Family Ties	186
Ding Dong	188
Hired Hand	189
The Hotcakes	191
The Nudist Colony	192
Repeat Offender	194
Carmen	195
A New Plan	196
All It Takes	197
Next!	198
Dad's Lamp	199
Overdose	200
Voices	201
Sizing It Up	202
Sex Signals	203
It Wasn't Me	204
Quid Pro Quo	206
Bang!	207
Personal Ad	208
Female Pharmacy	210
Number Four	212
A Small Problem	213
Because He Can't	214
Good Job	215
Wedded Bliss	216
Reminiscing	217

Liquor Up Front, Poker in the Rear

Plan B 218
Don't Ask Don't Tell 219
Fucked Again 220
Go For the Gold 221
Far Away 222
Cut the Schlitz 223
Gone Fishing 224
Bad Karma 225
At the Market 227
The New Maid 228
Dead Wood 230
On Vacation 231
Chinese Doctor 232
All Over Tan 234
Just Relax 236
Kiss of Life 238
Proud Papa 239
Going Postal 240
Money Talks 241
It's Your Choice 242

Liquor Up Front, Poker in the Rear

Liquor Up Front, Poker in the Rear

THE BEST MEDICINE

Laughter and sex are undoubtedly two of the best medicines for your health. They both help keep you fit and healthy! Several studies have proven that each of them can protect you from heart attacks. After a good laugh, or a good lay, you feel much more relaxed and calm. They recharge your energy, increase your productivity, and enable you to stay focused. Plus they reduce stress, and thus make you feel better!

It is very important to laugh out loud several times a day in order to minimize the effects of stress and maximize fun and humor in your life. It is equally important to have regular sexual encounters… but a word of caution. Don't do them both at the same time… or your partner may develop a complex!

Liquor Up Front, Poker in the Rear

Liquor Up Front, Poker in the Rear

Liquor Up Front, Poker in the Rear

Liquor Up Front, Poker in the Rear

VOODOO PENIS

A businessman was getting ready to go on a long business trip. He knew his wife was a flirtatious sort with an extremely healthy sex drive, so he thought he'd better buy her a little something to keep her occupied while he was gone.

He went to a store that sold sex toys and started looking around for something special to please her, and started talking to the old man behind the counter.

He explained his situation. The old man said, "Well, we have vibrating dildos, special attachments, and so on, but I don't know of anything that will keep her occupied for *weeks*, except..." and he stopped.

"Except what?" the man asked.

"Nothing, nothing."

"C'mon, tell me! I need something!"

"Well, sir, I don't usually mention this, but there is something called the Voodoo

Liquor Up Front, Poker in the Rear

Penis."

"So what's so special about this Voodoo Penis?" he asked.

The old man reached under the counter and pulled out a very old wooden box, carved with strange symbols and erotic images. He opened it, and there lay an ordinary-looking dildo.

The businessman laughed, and said, "Big damn deal. It looks like every other dildo in this shop!"

The old man replied, "But you haven't seen what it'll do yet." He pointed to a door and said, "Voodoo Penis, the door!"

The Voodoo Penis miraculously rose out of its box, darted over to the door, and started pounding the keyhole. The whole door shook wildly with the vibrations, so much so that a crack began to form down the middle.

Before the door split, the old man said "Voodoo Penis, return to box!"

The Voodoo Penis stopped, levitated back to the box, and lay there quietly once more.

"I'll take it!" said the businessman.

Liquor Up Front, Poker in the Rear

The guy took it home to his wife, told her it was a special dildo, and that to use it all she had to do was say "Voodoo Penis, my pussy!"

After he'd been gone a few days the wife was unbearably horny, and remembered the Voodoo Penis. She undressed, opened the box and said "Voodoo Penis, my pussy!"

The Voodoo Penis shot to her crotch and started pumping away. It was absolutely incredible, and was like nothing she had ever experienced before. After three mind-shattering orgasms she became exhausted, and decided she'd had enough.

She tried to pull it out, but it was stuck in her, still thrusting. She tried and tried to get it out, but nothing worked. Her husband had forgotten to tell her how to shut it off!

Worried, she decided to go to the hospital to see if they could help. She put her clothes on, got in the car, and started to drive, quivering with every thrust of the dildo. On the way, another incredibly intense orgasm made her swerve all over the road.

A police officer saw this and immediately

Liquor Up Front, Poker in the Rear

pulled her over. He asked for her license, and then asked how much she'd had to drink.

Gasping and twitching, she explained, "I haven't had *anything* to drink, officer. You see, I've got this Voodoo Penis thing stuck in my vagina, and it won't stop screwing me!"

The officer looked at her for a second, shook his head, and in an arrogant voice replied, "Yeah, right... Voodoo Penis, my *ass...!*"

MEDICAL CONDITION

A wealthy hospital benefactor was visiting the new wing she had financed when, during her tour, she passed a room where a male patient was masturbating.

"Oh my God!" screamed the woman. "That's disgraceful! Why is he doing that?"

The doctor who was leading the tour explained, "I am very sorry, but this man has a serious condition where the testicles rapidly fill with semen. If he doesn't do that five times a day, they'll explode and he'll die within minutes."

"Oh, well in that case, I guess it's okay," commented the woman.

In the very next room they saw a female nurse performing oral sex on a different male patient. Again the woman screamed, "Oh my God! How can *that* be justified?"

The doctor replied, "Same illness... better health plan!"

SIDE EFFECTS

A woman went to her doctor for a follow-up visit after the doctor had prescribed testosterone for her because she was a little worried about some of the side effects she was experiencing.

"Doctor, the hormones you've been giving me have really helped, but I'm afraid that you're giving me too much. I've started growing hair in places that I've never grown hair before."

The doctor reassured her. "A little hair growth is a perfectly normal side effect of testosterone. Just where has this hair appeared?"

"On my balls!"

DID YOU JUMP?

A young man joined the Army and signed up with the paratroopers. He went though the standard training, completed the practice jumps from higher and higher structures, and finally went to make his first jump from an airplane. The next day he called home to tell his father about it.

"So, did you jump?" the father asked.

"Well, let me tell you what happened. We got up in the plane, and the sergeant opened up the door and asked for volunteers. About a dozen men got up and just walked out of the plane!"

"Is that when you jumped?" asked the father.

"Um, not yet. Then the sergeant started to grab the other men one at a time and throw them out the door."

"Did you jump then?" asked the father.

"I'm getting to that. Everyone else had jumped, and I was the last man left on the

Liquor Up Front, Poker in the Rear

plane. I told the sergeant that I was too scared to jump. He told me to get off the plane or he'd kick my ass."

"So, did you jump?"

"Not then. He tried to push me out of the plane, but I grabbed onto the door and refused to go. Finally he called over to the Jump Master. The Jump Master is this great big guy, about six-foot five, and 250 pounds. He said to me, 'Boy, are you gonna jump or not?'"

"I said, 'No, sir. I'm too scared.'"

"So the Jump Master pulled down his zipper and took his penis out. I swear, it was about ten inches long and as big around as a baseball bat! He said, 'Boy, either you jump out that door, or I'm sticking this baby up your ass!'"

"So... did you jump?" asked the father.

"Well, a little, at first..."

THE SECOND TIME

After his exam the doctor said to the elderly man, "You appear to be in good health. Do you have any medical concerns you would like to ask me about?"

"In fact, I do," said the old man. "After I have sex with my wife, the first time I am usually hot and sweaty, and then, after I have sex with her the *second* time, I am usually cold and chilly."

After examining his elderly wife, the doctor said, "Everything appears to be fine. Do you have any medical concerns that you would like to discuss with me?" The lady replied that she had no questions or concerns.

The doctor then said to her, "Your husband had an unusual concern. He claims that he is usually hot and sweaty after having sex with you the first time, and then cold and chilly after the second time. Do you know why?"

Liquor Up Front, Poker in the Rear

"Oh that crazy old fart..." she replied. "That's because the *first* time is usually in August, and the *second* time is in January!"

Liquor Up Front, Poker in the Rear

FLAT TUMMY

A little boy walked into his parent's room and saw his mom bouncing up and down on top of his dad. The mom heard her son come in and quickly dismounted, worried about what he had seen. She dressed quickly and went to find him.

When the boy saw his mom he asked, "What were you and daddy doing?"

The mother replied, "Well you know your dad has a big tummy, and sometimes I have to get on top of it to help flatten it.

"You're wasting your time," said the boy.

"Why is that?" asked his mom, puzzled.

"Well, when you go shopping, the lady next door comes over, gets on her knees and blows it right back up!"

LITTLE SOLDIER

When a man walked into a supermarket with his zipper down, a lady cashier walked up to him and said, "Excuse me sir, your barracks door is open."

This is not a phrase women normally used, so he went on his way looking a bit puzzled. When he was about done shopping, a man came up and said, "Hey, your fly is open."

He zipped up, finished his shopping, and intentionally got into line to check out with the lady was who had told him about his "barracks door." He was planning to have a little fun with her.

When he reached her counter he said, "When you saw my barracks door open, did you see a soldier standing at attention?"

The lady thought for a moment and said, "No, no, I didn't. All I saw was a disabled veteran sitting on two old duffel bags…"

POKER PLAYER

Two couples were playing poker one evening when John accidentally dropped some cards on the floor. When he bent down under the table to pick them up he noticed that Bill's wife, Sue, wasn't wearing any panties under her dress!

Shocked by this, John tried to sit back up again, but hit his head on the table and emerged red-faced. Later, he went to the kitchen to get some refreshments.

Bill's wife followed and asked, "Did you see anything that you liked under there?"

Surprised by her boldness, John courageously admitted that, yes indeed, he most certainly had.

She said, "Well, you can have it - but it will cost you five hundred dollars."

After taking a minute or two to assess the financial and moral costs of this offer, John confirmed that he was interested. She told him that since her husband Bill worked

Liquor Up Front, Poker in the Rear

Friday afternoons and John didn't, he should be at her house around two o'clock at the end of the week.

When Friday rolled around John showed up at Bill's house at two o'clock sharp, and after paying Sue the agreed sum they went to the bedroom and closed the deal. Afterwards, John quickly dressed and left.

As usual Bill came home from work at six, and upon entering the house asked his wife abruptly, "Did John come by the house today?"

With a lump in her throat Sue answered, "Why yes, he did stop by for a few minutes this afternoon."

Her heart nearly skipped a beat when her husband curtly asked, "And did he give you five hundred dollars?"

In terror, she assumed that somehow he had found out - and after mustering her best poker face replied, "Well, yes, as a matter of fact he did."

Bill, with a satisfied look on his face, surprised his wife by saying, "Good, I was hoping he did. John came by the office this

Liquor Up Front, Poker in the Rear

morning and borrowed the money from me, and promised he'd stop by this afternoon on his way home and pay me back."

Now THAT is a poker player!

Liquor Up Front, Poker in the Rear

CHRISTMAS PARTY

Tom had been in the liquor business for twenty-five years. Finally sick of the stress, he quit his job and bought fifty acres of land in Alaska as far from humanity as possible. He saw the postman once a week, and got groceries once a month. Otherwise, it was total peace and quiet.

After six months or so of almost total isolation someone knocked on his door. He opened it and saw a huge, bearded man standing there.

"Name's Lars, your neighbor from forty miles up the road. I'm having a Christmas party Friday night, and thought you might like to come."

"Great," said Tom, "after six months out here I'm ready to meet some of the local folks. Thank you."

As Lars was leaving he stopped and said, "Gotta warn you... there's gonna be some drinkin'."

Liquor Up Front, Poker in the Rear

"Not a problem," said Tom. "After twenty-five years in the liquor business, I can drink with the best of 'em."

Again, the big man started to leave and stopped. "More 'n likely gonna be some fightin' too."

"Well, I get along with people, I'll be all right. I'll be there. Thanks again."

"More'n likely be some wild sex, too."

"Now that's really not a problem," said Tom, warming to the idea. "I've been all alone for six months! I'll *definitely* be there. By the way, what should I wear?"

"Whatever you want. Just gonna be the two of us…"

COWBOY UP

Two Texans were out on the range talking about their favorite sex positions. One said, "I think I enjoy the rodeo position the best."

"I don't think I have ever heard of that one," said the other cowboy. "What is it?"

"Well, it's where you get your wife down on all fours and you mount her from behind. Then you reach around and cup one of her breasts in each hand and whisper in her ear, 'Boy, these feel just like your sister's.' Then you try and stay on for eight seconds!"

I HAVE A PLAN

Shamus and Murphy fancied a pint or two, but didn't have a lot of money. Between them, they could only raise the staggering sum of fifty pence.

Murphy said, "Hang on, I have an idea." He went next door to the butcher's shop, and came out with one large sausage.

Shamus said, "Are you crazy? Now we don't have any money left at all!"

Murphy replied, "Don't worry laddy, just follow me."

They went into the first pub they saw, where Murphy happily ordered two pints of Guinness and two glasses of Jameson Whisky.

Shamus said, "Now you've really lost it! Do you know the trouble we'll be in? We haven't got any money!"

Murphy replied with a smile, "Don't you worry, lad, I have a plan. Cheers!"

They downed their drinks, and Murphy

Liquor Up Front, Poker in the Rear

said, "Okay, I'll stick the sausage through my zipper, and you go down on your knees and put it in your mouth." Just as Murphy had planned the barman noticed them, went berserk, and threw them out.

They continued doing this, pub after pub, getting more and more drunk – and all for free. At the tenth pub Shamus said, "Murphy, I don't think I can do any more o' this. I'm drunk, and me knees are killin' me!"

Murphy said, "How do you think I feel? I lost the bloody sausage in the third pub!"

Liquor Up Front, Poker in the Rear

ALWAYS TELL THE TRUTH

A married man was having an affair with his secretary. One day their passions overcame them and they took off for her house, where they made passionate love all afternoon. Exhausted from the wild sex, they fell asleep and awakened around eight that evening. As the man threw on his clothes, he told the woman to take his shoes outside and rub them in the grass and dirt. Mystified, she nonetheless complied. He then slipped into his shoes and drove home.

"Where have you been?" demanded his wife when he entered the house.

"Darling, I can't lie to you. I've been having an affair with my secretary, and we've been having sex all afternoon. I fell asleep, and didn't wake up until eight o'clock."

The wife glanced down at his shoes and said, "You lying bastard! You've been playing golf again!"

FAMILY RESEMBLANCE

There was a middle aged couple that had two stunningly beautiful teenage daughters who decided to try one last time for the son they had always wanted. After months of trying the wife finally got pregnant, and sure enough delivered a healthy baby boy nine months later. The joyful father rushed into the nursery to see his new son, took one look, and was horrified to see the ugliest child he had ever seen. He went to his wife and told her there was no possible way he could be the father of that child.

"Look at the two beautiful daughters I fathered!" Then he gave her a stern look and asked, "Have you been fooling around on me?"

The wife just smiled sweetly and said, "Well, not *this* time!"

PRIVATE PARTS

A mortician was working late one night examining dead bodies before they were sent off to be buried. As he examined the body of Mr. Schwartz, who was about to be cremated, he was amazed. Schwartz had the longest penis he had ever seen!

"I'm sorry, Mr. Schwartz," said the mortician, "but I can't send you off to be cremated with such a tremendously huge tallywacker as this. It has to be saved for posterity."

With that, the coroner used his tools to remove the dead man's unit. He then stuffed his prize into a briefcase and took it home. The first person he showed it to was his wife.

"I have something to show you that you won't believe," he said as he opened up his briefcase.

"Oh my God!" the wife suddenly screamed, "Schwartz is dead!"

COMMON COURTESY

A woman was in bed with her lover when she heard her husband opening the front door.

"Hurry," she said, "stand in the corner, and don't move."

She then quickly rubbed baby oil all over his body and dusted him with some talcum powder.

"Don't move a muscle until I tell you to," she whispered. "Just pretend you're a statue."

"What's this, honey?" the husband inquired as he entered the room.

"Oh... it's just a statue," she replied nonchalantly. "The Smiths bought one for their bedroom, and I liked it so much I got one for us too."

No more was said about the statue, not even later when they went to sleep. Around two in the morning the husband got out of bed, went to the kitchen, and returned a

Liquor Up Front, Poker in the Rear

while later with a sandwich and a glass of milk.

"Here," he said to the statue, "eat something. I stood like an idiot at the Smith's for three days, and nobody offered me so much as a glass of water!"

TIT FOR TAT

A man walked into a nightclub one night, went up to the bar, and asked for a beer.

"Certainly sir, that'll be one cent."

"One cent?!" exclaimed the man. "That's unbelievable!"

The man then glanced at the menu and asked, "Could I have a nice juicy T-bone steak, with chips, peas and a fried egg?"

"Certainly, sir," replied the barman, "but that comes to real money."

"How much?" inquired the man.

"*Four* cents," the bartender replied.

"Four Cents?!" exclaimed the surprised man. "Where's the guy who owns this place?"

The bartender replied, "He's upstairs with my wife."

The man asked, "What's he doing upstairs with your wife?"

The bartender replied, "Basically, the same thing I'm doing to his business!"

FINAL CONFESSION

As Jake was dying, his wife Becky was maintaining a vigil by his side. She held his fragile hand, tears running down her face, and her praying roused him from his slumber. He looked up, and his pale lips began to move slightly.

"Becky my darling," he whispered.

"Hush my love," she said. "Rest... don't try to talk."

He was insistent. "Becky," he said in his tired voice, "I must confess something."

"There's nothing to confess," replied the weeping Becky, "everything's all right. Now go to sleep."

"No... I can't. I must die in peace, Becky. I must tell you... I slept with your sister, your best friend, her best friend... and your mother!"

"Yes, I know my darling," whispered Becky. "Now just close your eyes, and let the poison work."

Liquor Up Front, Poker in the Rear

NIGHT ON THE TOWN

Two old men who were feeling close to their last days on earth decided to have a last night on the town. After a few drinks, they ended up at the local brothel.

The madam took one look at the two geezers and whispered to her manager, "Go up to the first two rooms and put an inflated doll on each bed. I'm not wasting two of my girls on them. These two are so old and drunk they won't know the difference."

The two men went up the stairs and took care of their business. As they were walking home afterward the first one said, "You know, I think my girl was dead!"

"Dead?" said his friend, "Why would you think that?"

"Well, she never moved or made a sound all the time I was loving her…"

His friend said, "That's nothing. I think mine was a witch!"

"A witch? Why would you say that?"

Liquor Up Front, Poker in the Rear

"Well, I was making love to her and kissing her neck, and when I gave it a little bite... she farted and flew right out the damn window!"

Liquor Up Front, Poker in the Rear

DROP THE SOAP

Two priests were off to the showers late one night, and had undressed and stepped into the stalls before they realized there was no soap. Father John said he had some soap in his room and went to get it, not bothering to dress.

He grabbed two bars of soap, one in each hand, and headed back to the showers. He was halfway down the hall when he saw three nuns heading his way. Having no place to hide, he stood against the wall and froze like a statue.

The nuns stopped and commented on how lifelike he looked.

Then the first nun suddenly reached out and pulled on his manhood.

Startled, he dropped a bar of soap.

"Oh look," said the first nun, "it's a soap dispenser."

To test her theory, the second nun also pulled on his manhood... and sure enough,

Liquor Up Front, Poker in the Rear

he dropped the second bar of soap.

Then the third nun decided to have a go.

She pulled once, then twice, and three times - but nothing happened. Frustrated, she gave several more tugs, and then finally yelled, "Mary, Mother of God - hand lotion too!"

Liquor Up Front, Poker in the Rear

SEX FROG

A beautiful, well endowed young blonde went to her local pet store in search of an exotic pet. As she looked about the store, she noticed a box full of frogs. The sign said:

Sex Frogs! $20 each! Comes with Money Back Guarantee! (Complete instructions included).

The girl excitedly looked around to see if anybody was watching her, and whispered softly to the man behind the counter, "I'll take one."

The man packaged the frog and said, "Make sure to follow the instructions carefully." The girl nodded, grabbed the box, and was quickly on her way home. As soon as she closed the door to her apartment she took out the instructions, read them thoroughly, and did exactly what it said to do:

Liquor Up Front, Poker in the Rear

1. *Take a shower.*

2. *Splash on some nice smelling perfume.*

3. *Slip into a very sexy teddy.*

4. *Crawl into bed and put the frog down "there."*

She then quickly got into bed with the frog, and to her surprise nothing happened! The girl was totally frustrated, and quite upset at this point. She then re-read the instructions and noticed at the bottom of the paper it said, "If you have any problems or questions, please call the pet store."

So she called the pet store. The man said, "I had some other complaints earlier today. I'll be right over!"

Within five minutes the man was ringing her doorbell. The girl welcomed him in and said, "I've done everything according to the instructions, and the damn thing just sits there."

The man, looking very concerned, picked up the frog, stared directly into its eyes and sternly said, "Listen to me! I'm only going to show you how to do this *one* more time!"

TRUE CONFESSION

A cabbie picked up a Nun, and when she got into the cab the driver wouldn't stop staring at her. She asked him why he was staring, and he replied, "I have a question to ask, but I don't want to offend you."

She answered, "My son, you cannot offend me. When you're as old as I am and have been a nun as long as I have, you get a chance to see and hear just about everything. I'm sure that there's nothing you could say or ask that I would find offensive."

"Well, I've always fantasized about having a nun kiss me."

She responded, "Well, let's see what we can do about that. Number one, you have to be single, and number two, you must be Catholic."

The cab driver was very excited and said, "Yes, I'm single, and I'm Catholic!"

"Okay then," the nun said. "Pull into the next alley." The nun fulfilled his fantasy

Liquor Up Front, Poker in the Rear

with a kiss that would make a hooker blush, but when they got back on the road the cab driver started crying.

"My dear child," said the nun, "why are you crying?"

"Forgive me, but I've sinned. I lied. I must confess – I'm married, and I'm really Jewish."

The nun said, "That's okay. My name is Kevin, and I'm on my way to a Halloween party!"

Liquor Up Front, Poker in the Rear

NO MORE FOR YOU!

A little boy went down to breakfast. Since his family lived on a farm, his mother asked if he had done his chores. "Not yet," he replied.

His mother told him there would be no breakfast until he did them. He was a little upset, so as he went to feed the chickens he kicked one. Then, as he went to feed the cows, he kicked one of them. Finally, as he went to feed the pigs, he kicked one of them.

When he went back in for breakfast his mother gave him just a bowl of dry cereal.

"How come I don't get any eggs and bacon? And why don't I have any milk in my cereal?" he asked.

"Well," his mother said, "I saw you kick a *chicken*, so you don't get any *eggs* for a week. I saw you kick the *pig*, so you don't get any *bacon* for a week either. I also saw you kick the *cow*, so for a week you aren't getting any *milk*."

Liquor Up Front, Poker in the Rear

Just then his father came down for breakfast, obviously in a bad mood, and kicked the cat halfway across the kitchen.

The little boy looked up at his mother with a smile and said, "Are you going to tell him, or shall I?"

FROZEN SKUNK

A man and his wife were driving home one very cold night when the wife asks her husband to stop the car. There was a baby skunk lying at the side of the road, and she got out to see if it was still alive.

It was, and she said to her husband, "It's nearly frozen to death. Can we take it with us, get it warm, and let it go in the morning?"

He said, "Okay. Get in the car with it."

"Where shall I put it to get it warm?"

He says, "Put it in between your legs. It's nice and warm there."

"But what about the smell?" she asked.

"It'll be okay. Just hold its nose!" he replied.

The man is expected to recover, but the skunk she beat him with died at the scene.

Liquor Up Front, Poker in the Rear

MOBY DICK'S SON

Two whales, a male and a female, were swimming side by side in the ocean. Suddenly the male whale spotted a ship in the distance and recognized it as the whaling ship that killed his father.

Filled with anger, he said to his female companion, "That's the ship that killed my father! Let's swim closer!"

When they were close enough the male said, "Why don't we swim under the ship and blow air through our blow holes and break it into a million pieces? That will be sweet revenge."

The female agreed.

They each took a deep breath of air, swam underwater, and blew enormous amounts of air under the hull. The ship flew into the air, crashed back to the sea, and broke into a million pieces.

The pair of whales started to swim off when they realized that the sailors were not

Liquor Up Front, Poker in the Rear

dead, but were instead clinging to pieces of wood floating in the ocean.

The male whale was furious, and said to the female whale, "They're still alive, but I've got another idea. Let's swim around and gobble up all the sailors!"

That's when the female stopped swimming, looked at the male and said, "Oh no... I agreed to the blow job, but I'm NOT swallowing *any* seamen!"

THE RICH HOOKER

A guy was walking along the strip in Las Vegas when a knockout looking hooker caught his eye. He struck up a conversation, and eventually asked the hooker, "How much do you charge?"

Hooker replied, "It starts at five hundred dollars for a hand-job."

The guy said, "Five hundred dollars! For a hand-job! No hand-job is worth *that* kind of money!"

The hooker said, "Do you see that Denny's on the corner?"

"Yes."

"Do you see the Denny's about a block further down?"

"Yes."

"And beyond that, do you see that third Denny's?"

"Yes."

"Well," said the hooker, smiling invitingly, "I own them... and I own them

Liquor Up Front, Poker in the Rear

because I give a hand-job that's worth five hundred dollars."

The guy said, "What the hell? You only live once. I'll give it a try," and they retired to a nearby motel.

A short time later the guy was sitting on the bed, realizing that he just experienced the hand-job of a lifetime, worth every bit of five hundred dollars. He was so amazed he said, "I suppose a blow-job is a thousand dollars?"

The hooker replied, "Fifteen hundred."

"I wouldn't pay that for a blow-job!"

The hooker replied, "Step over here to the window, big boy. Do you see that casino just across the street? I own it outright... and I own it because I give a blow-job that's worth every cent of fifteen hundred dollars."

The guy, basking in the afterglow of that terrific hand-job, decided to put off the new car for another year or so and said, "Okay, sign me up!"

Twenty minutes later he was sitting on the bed, more amazed than before. He could scarcely believe it, but he felt he had truly

Liquor Up Front, Poker in the Rear

gotten his money's worth. He then decided to dip into the retirement savings for one last glorious and unforgettable experience.

He then asked the hooker, "How much for some pussy?"

The hooker said, "Come over here to the window, I want to show you something. Do you see how the whole city of Las Vegas is laid out before us, all those beautiful lights, the gambling palaces, and the showplaces?"

"Damn!" the guy said in awe, "You own the whole city?"

"No," the hooker replied, "but I *would* if I *had* a pussy!"

ELDER SEX

A Florida couple, both well into their seventies, went to a sex therapist's office.

The doctor asked, "What can I do for you?"

The man said, "Will you watch us have sexual intercourse?"

The doctor raised both eyebrows, but was so amazed that such an elderly couple was asking for sexual advice that he agreed.

When the couple finished the doctor said, "There's absolutely nothing wrong with the way you have intercourse." He thanked them for coming, wished them good luck, charged them fifty dollars, and said goodbye.

The next week the couple returned and asked the sex therapist to watch again. He was a bit puzzled, but agreed.

This happened several weeks in a row. The couple made an appointment, had intercourse with no problems, paid the

Liquor Up Front, Poker in the Rear

doctor, and then left. Finally, after five or six weeks of this routine the doctor said, "I'm sorry, but I have to ask. Just what are you trying to find out?"

The old man said, "We're not trying to find out anything. She's married, and we can't go to her house. I'm married, so we can't go to mine. The Holiday Inn charges ninety-eight dollars. The Hilton charges two hundred. But we can do it here for fifty dollars - and I get forty-three back from Medicare!"

Liquor Up Front, Poker in the Rear

SENSITIVITY TEST FOR MEN

1. In the company of females, intercourse should be referred to as:

A. Lovemaking.
B. Screwing.
C. Taking the pigskin bus to tuna town.

2. You should make love to a woman for the first time only after you've shared:

A. Your views about what you expect from a sexual relationship.
B. Your blood-test results.
C. Five tequila slammers.

3. You should time your orgasm so that:

A. Your partner climaxes first.
B. You both climax simultaneously.
C. You don't miss ESPN Sports Center.

Liquor Up Front, Poker in the Rear

4. Passionate, spontaneous sex on the kitchen floor is:

A. Healthy, creative love-play.
B. Not the sort of thing your wife/girlfriend would agree to.
C. Not the sort of thing your wife/girlfriend needs to ever find out about.

5. Spending the whole night cuddling a woman you've just had sex with is:

A. The best part of the experience.
B. The second best part of the experience.
C. One hundred dollars extra.

6. Your wife says she's gained five pounds in the last month. You tell her it:

A. Does not influence your affection for her.
B. Is not a problem, she can join your gym.
C. Is a conservative estimate.

Liquor Up Front, Poker in the Rear

7. You think today's sensitive man is:

A. A myth.

B. An oxymoron.

C. A moron.

8. Foreplay is to sex as:

A. An appetizer is to entree.

B. Primer is to paint.

C. A long line is to an amusement park ride.

9. Which of the following are you most likely to find yourself saying at the end of a relationship?

A. "I hope we can still be friends."

B. "I'm not in right now, please leave a message at the beep."

C. "Dumpsville, population YOU."

10. A woman who is uncomfortable watching you masturbate:

A. Probably needs a little more time before she can cope with that sort of intimacy.

B. Is uptight and a waste of time.

C. Shouldn't have sat near you on the bus!

Liquor Up Front, Poker in the Rear

THE PICKLE SLICER

Yossel Zelkovitz worked in a pickle factory, and for many years had a powerful desire to put his penis in the pickle slicer.

Unable to stand it any longer, he sought professional help. After six months his therapist gave up and advised Yossel to go ahead and do it, or he would probably never have peace of mind.

The next day he came home from work very early. His wife Sarah became alarmed, and wanted to know what had happened. Yossel tearfully confessed his tormenting desire, and went on to explain that today he finally went ahead and did it and was immediately fired from his job.

Sarah gasped and quickly yanked down his pants and boxer shorts - only to find a normal, completely intact penis.

She looked up and said, "I... I don't understand. What about the pickle slicer?"

Yossel replied, "I think she got fired too!"

Liquor Up Front, Poker in the Rear

BALL FOUR

An Irishman immigrated to the USA and attended his first baseball game. The first batter approached the batter's box, took a few swings, and then hit a double. Everyone was on their feet screaming, "Run! Run!"

The next batter hit a single. The Irishman listened as the crowd again cheered, "RUN! RUN!" The Irishman was enjoying the game, and began screaming with the fans.

The fifth batter came up and drew a walk. The umpire called, "Take your base!" The batter started his slow trot to first base, and he Irishman screamed, "Rrrrun ye lazy bastard, rrrun!"

The people around him begin laughing. Embarrassed, the Irishman sat back down.

A friendly fan, noting the man's embarrassment, leaned over and said, "He doesn't have to run – he's got four balls."

So the Irishman stood up and screamed, "Walk with *pride*, laddie, walk with *pride!*"

Liquor Up Front, Poker in the Rear

LITTLE BLUE PILL

An older man went to the doctor and asked for a prescription for Viagra. The physician looked him over and said, "Viagra can be very dangerous, and we don't dispense it indiscriminately. Bring your wife to my office next week and we'll discuss this in detail."

The following week the man showed up with his wife. The doctor asked to see the wife by herself for a few moments, and she followed him back to the examining room.

The doctor asked her to disrobe, and she did. He then asked her to turn around 360 degrees a few times, and instructed her to get up on the examining table and get into various positions. He then told her she could get dressed and went out to meet the male patient.

"Sir," the doctor said, "There is nothing wrong with you. I couldn't get an erection either!"

HOLY HOT DOGS

Two Irish nuns had just arrived in the USA by boat, and one said to the other, "I hear that the people in this country actually eat dogs."

"That's odd," her companion replied, "but if we shall live in America, we might as well do as the Americans do."

Nodding emphatically, the mother superior pointed to a hot dog vendor and they both walked towards the cart.

"Two dogs, please," said one.

The vendor was only too pleased to oblige, and wrapped both hot dogs in foil and handed them over the counter. Excited, the nuns hurried over to a bench and began to unwrap their 'dogs.'

The mother superior was first to open hers. She began to blush and then, staring at it for a moment, leaned over to the other nun and whispered cautiously, "What part did *you* get?"

Liquor Up Front, Poker in the Rear

TWO BROTHERS

There were once two brothers. One was very good and always tried to live right and be helpful to others. His brother on the other hand was bad, did all the things that men should not do in life, and didn't care who he hurt.

Then one day the bad brother died. He was still missed by his brother, since he loved him despite his ways.

Finally, years later, the good brother also died and went to Heaven. Everything was beautiful and wonderful there, and he was very happy.

One day he asked God where his brother was, as he hadn't seen him. God said that he was sorry, but his brother had lived a terrible life and had gone to Hell instead.

The good brother then asked God if there was any way for him to see his brother, and God gave him the power of vision so he could see into Hell - and there was his

Liquor Up Front, Poker in the Rear

brother, sitting on a bench with a keg of beer under one arm and a gorgeous blonde on the other.

Confused, the good brother said to God, "I am so happy that you let me into Heaven with you. It is so beautiful here and I love it. But I don't understand - if my brother was bad enough to go to Hell, why does he have the keg of beer and a gorgeous blonde? It hardly seems like a punishment."

God said unto him, "Things are not always as they seem, my son. The keg has no hole in it, and the blonde doesn't either!"

QUICK THINKING

A man boarded an airplane and took his seat. As he settled in he glanced up and saw an unusually beautiful woman boarding the plane, and soon realized she was heading straight toward his seat. Lo and behold, she took the seat right beside his.

Eager to strike up a conversation, he blurted out, "Business trip, or vacation?"

She turned, smiled and said, "Business... the Annual Sexual Education Convention in Chicago."

He swallowed hard. Here was the most gorgeous woman he had ever seen sitting next to him, and she was going to a meeting for sex education!

Struggling to maintain his composure, he calmly asked, "What's your role at this convention?"

"Lecturer," she responded. "I use my experience to debunk some of the popular myths about sexuality."

Liquor Up Front, Poker in the Rear

"Really," he said. "What myths are those?"

"Well," she explained... "one popular myth is that African-American men are the best endowed, when in fact it's the Native American Indian who is most likely to possess that trait. Another popular myth is that French men are the best lovers, when actually it is men of Jewish descent. We have also found that the best potential lover in all categories is the Southern Redneck."

Suddenly the woman became a little uncomfortable, and blushed.

"I'm sorry," she said. "I shouldn't really be discussing this with you. I don't even know your name."

"Tonto," the man said. "Tonto Goldstein. But my friends call me Bubba!"

Liquor Up Front, Poker in the Rear

CLOSE CALL

Three girls worked in an office with the same female boss, and each day they noticed that the boss left work early.

One day the three girls decided that when their boss left, they would leave shortly after her. After all, she never came back to work - so she would never know they had gone home early too.

The brunette was thrilled to be home early. She did a little gardening, spent time playing with her son, and enjoyed her evening.

The redhead was pleased to be able to get in a quick workout at the spa before meeting a dinner date.

The blonde was happy to get home early and surprise her husband, but when she got to her bedroom she heard noises coming from inside. Slowly and quietly she cracked open the door, and was mortified to see her husband in bed with her boss. Gently, she

Liquor Up Front, Poker in the Rear

closed the door and crept out of her house.

The next day during their coffee break the brunette and redhead planned to leave early again, and asked the blonde if she was going to do likewise.

"No *way*," the blonde exclaimed. "I almost got caught yesterday!"

TEXAS WOMAN

A West Texas cowboy's wife came home just in time to find her husband in bed with another woman. With the super-human strength borne of fury and cutting calves, she dragged him down the stairs, out the back door, and into the tool shed out in back of the barn.

She put his tally-whacker in a vice, secured it tightly, and removed the handle. Next she picked up an old carpenter's saw. The banged up cowboy was terrified and hollered, "Stop! Stop! You're not gonna cut it off with that rusty damn saw, are you?"

The wife, with a gleam of revenge in her eye, put the saw in her husband's hand and said, "Nope. I'm gonna set this old shed on fire, and go to town for a cold beer. You can do whatever you want..."

JACK AND DEBRA

The boss was in quandary. The company was down-sizing, and he had to fire somebody in the office.

He had it narrowed down to one of two people - Debra or Jack. It was an impossible decision, since they were both super workers.

Rather than flip a coin, he decided he would fire the first one who used the water cooler the next morning.

Debra came in the next morning with a horrible hang-over after partying all night, and went to the cooler to take an aspirin.

The boss approached her and said, "Debra, I've never had to do this before, but I have to lay you or Jack off."

"Could you please jack off?" she said. "I feel like *shit* this morning..."

Liquor Up Front, Poker in the Rear

THE TOAST

John O'Reilly hoisted his beer and said, "Here's to spending the rest of me life, between the legs of me beautiful wife!"

That won him the top prize at the pub for the best toast of the night!

He went home and told his wife, Mary, "I won the prize for the best toast of the night."

She said, "Aye, did ye now. And what was your toast?"

John said, "Here's to spending the rest of me life, sitting in church beside me beautiful wife."

"Oh, that is very nice indeed, John!" Mary said.

The next day Mary ran into one of John's drinking buddies on the street corner. The man chuckled leeringly and said, "John won the prize the other night at the pub with a toast about you, Mary."

She said, "Aye, he told me, and I must say I was a bit surprised. You know, he's only

Liquor Up Front, Poker in the Rear

been there twice in the last four years. Once he fell asleep, and the other time I had to pull him by the ears to make him come!"

Liquor Up Front, Poker in the Rear

THE FACE LIFT

A middle-aged woman decided to have a face-lift for her birthday. She spent eight thousand dollars, and felt great about the results. On her way home, she stopped at a news stand to buy a newspaper.

Before leaving she said to the clerk, "I hope you don't mind my asking, but how old do you think I am?"

"About thirty-two," was the reply.

"I'm exactly forty-seven," the woman said happily.

A little while later she went into McDonald's and asked the counter girl, "How old do you think I am?"

"I guess about twenty-nine."

The woman excitedly replied, "Nope, I'm forty-seven!"

Now she was feeling really great about herself. On her way down the street, she asked everyone in sight her question.

While waiting for the bus to go home, she

Liquor Up Front, Poker in the Rear

asked an old retired man the same question.

He replied, "Lady, I'm seventy-eight and my eyesight is going... but when I was young, there was a sure way to tell how old a woman was. It sounds kind of forward, but it requires you to let me put my hands under your bra. Then I can tell you *exactly* how old you are."

They waited in silence on the empty street until curiosity got the best of her. She finally blurted out, "What the hell, go ahead."

The man slipped both of his hands under her blouse and under her bra and began to feel around very slowly and carefully.

After a couple of minutes of this she said, "Okay, that's enough... how old am I?"

The old man completed one last squeeze of her breasts, removed his hands and said, "Madam, you are forty-seven years old."

Stunned and amazed, the woman said, "That was incredible! How could you possibly know that from a feel of my breasts?"

The man replied, "It's simple. I was in line behind you at McDonald's!"

Liquor Up Front, Poker in the Rear

BABY TEXAN

A Texan was drinking in a New York bar when he got a call on his cell phone. He hung up grinning from ear to ear, ordered a round of drinks for everybody in the bar, and announced that his wife had produced a typical Texas baby boy weighing twenty-five pounds.

Nobody could believe that any new baby could weigh that much, but the Texan just shrugged, "That's about average down home, folks... like I said, my son's a typical Texas baby boy."

Congratulations showered him from all around, and there were many exclamations of, "WOW!" One woman even fainted due to sympathy pains.

Two weeks later he returned to the bar.

The bartender said, "Say, aren't you the father of that typical Texas baby that weighed twenty-five pounds at birth? Everybody's been making bets about how

Liquor Up Front, Poker in the Rear

big he'd be in two weeks. So, how much does he weigh now?"

The proud father answered, "Seventeen pounds."

The bartender was puzzled, concerned, and a little suspicious. "What happened? He already weighed twenty-five pounds the day he was born!"

The Texas father took a slow swig from his long-neck Lone Star beer, wiped his lips on his shirt sleeve, leaned toward the bartender and proudly said, "Yep, sure did. Had'm circumcised!"

Liquor Up Front, Poker in the Rear

SEXUAL HARRASSMENT

Every morning a man walked up to a woman in his office, stood very close to her, inhaled a big breath of air through his nose, and told her that her hair smelled nice.

After a week of this she couldn't stand it anymore and took her complaint to a supervisor in Human Resources.

Without identifying the guy, she explained what her co-worker was doing and stated that she wanted to file a sexual harassment grievance against him.

The Human Resources supervisor was puzzled by this request and asked, "What is sexually threatening about a co-worker telling you your hair smells nice?"

The woman replied, "It's Keith... the midget!"

Liquor Up Front, Poker in the Rear

OSAMA & THE GENIE

While trying to escape through Pakistan, Osama Bin Laden found a bottle on a beach and picked it up.

Suddenly, a female genie rose from the bottle and with a smile said, "Master, may I grant you one wish?"

"You ignorant, unworthy daughter-of-a-dog. Don't you know who I am? I don't need any common woman giving me anything!" barked Bin Laden.

The shocked genie said, "Please, I must grant you a wish or I will be returned to that bottle forever."

Osama thought a moment, then grumbled about the impertinence of the woman and said, "Very well, I want to awaken with three American women in my bed in the morning. Just do it and be off with you!"

The annoyed genie said, "So be it!" and disappeared.

The next morning Bin Laden woke up in

Liquor Up Front, Poker in the Rear

bed with Lorena Bobbitt, Tonya Harding, and Hillary Clinton... and his penis was gone, his knees were broken, and he had no health insurance!

FIRM IT UP

One morning a man walked up to his wife while she was making breakfast, pinched her on the butt and said, "You know, if you firmed up we could get rid of your control top panty hose."

While this was on the edge of intolerable, she kept silent.

The next morning, the man woke his wife with a pinch on each of her breasts and said, "You know, if you firmed these up we could get rid of your support bra."

This was beyond a silent response, so she rolled over and grabbed him by his penis.

With a death grip in place she said, "You know, if you firmed *this* up we could get rid of the gardener, the postman, the pool man, and your brother!"

NEWLYWEDS

Monte and his wife had only been married for two weeks. Although he was very much in love he couldn't wait to go out on the town and party with his old buddies, so he said to his new wife, "Honey, I'll be right back."

"Where are you going, coochy cooh?" asked Mrs. Monte.

"I'm going to the bar, pretty face. I'm going to have a beer."

She said, "You want a beer, my love?"

She opened the door to the refrigerator and showed him twenty-five different kinds of beer from a dozen different countries.

Monte didn't know what to do, and the only thing that he could think of saying was, "Yes, lollypop... but at the bar... you know, they have frozen glasses..."

He didn't get to finish the sentence, because the wife interrupted him by saying, "You want a frozen glass, puppy face?"

Liquor Up Front, Poker in the Rear

She took a huge beer mug out of the freezer, so frozen that she was getting 'nippley' just holding it.

Monte, looking a bit pale, said, "Yes, tootsie roll, but at the bar they have those hors d'oeuvres that are really delicious... I won't be long. I'll be right back. I promise. Okay?"

"You want hors d'oeuvres, poochi pooh?"

She opened the oven and took out five dishes of different hors d'oeuvres - chicken wings, pigs in blankets, mushroom caps, pork strips, and egg rolls.

"But my sweet honey... at the bar... you know... there's swearing... dirty words and all that... it kind of reminds me of my days in the Army."

"You want dirty words, cutie pie?... Okay... LISTEN UP, DICKHEAD! DRINK YOUR FUCKING BEER IN YOUR GODDAMN FROZEN MUG AND EAT YOUR MOTHERFUCKING SNACKS, BECAUSE YOU ARE MARRIED NOW, AND YOU AREN'T GOING *ANYWHERE!* GOT IT, ASSHOLE?"

Liquor Up Front, Poker in the Rear

NAG, NAG, NAG

An attorney got home late one evening after a very taxing day trying to get a stay of execution for his client, a man named Wilbur Wright, who was due to be hanged for murder at midnight. His last-minute plea for clemency to the Governor had failed, and he was feeling tired and depressed.

As soon as he got through the door his wife started on about, "What time of night do you call this? Where have you been?" and on and on...

Too shattered to play his usual role in this familiar ritual, he went and poured himself a very large whisky and headed off for a long hot soak in the bathtub... pursued by the predictable sarcastic remarks.

While he was in the bath the phone rang, which the wife answered and was told that her husband's client had been granted his stay of execution after all. Realizing what a day he must have had, she relented a little

Liquor Up Front, Poker in the Rear

and went upstairs to give him the good news.

As she opened the bathroom door she was greeted by the sight of her husband's rear view as he was bent over naked drying his legs and feet.

"They're not hanging Wright tonight!" she said.

The attorney whirled around and screamed hysterically, "For crying out loud woman, don't you *ever* stop *nagging!?*"

Liquor Up Front, Poker in the Rear

ALL ABOARD!

After returning from his honeymoon in Florida with his new bride Virginia, Luigi stopped by his old barbershop in Manhattan to say hello to his friends.

Giovanni said, "Hey Luigi, how wassah de treepa?"

Luigi said, "Everytinga wassah perfecto except for da traina ride down south."

"Whadda you mean, Luigi?" asked Giovanni.

"Well, we boarda da train at Granna Central Station. My beautiful Virginia, she packa a bigga basket a food. She broughta vino, some nicea cigars for me, and we were looking a forward to da trip. Everytinga wassah okey dokey until we getta hungry and open uppa da luncha basket. The conductore comma by, wagga hissa finger at us an say, 'No eat in dissa car. Musta use a dining car.'"

"So, me and my beautiful Virginia, we go

Liquor Up Front, Poker in the Rear

to dining car, eat a bigga luncha and start to open a bottle of nice vino! Conductore walka by again, waga hissa finger and say, 'No drinka in dissa car. Musta use a club a car.'"

"So, we go to club car. "While drinkin vino, I start to lighta my biga cigar. The conductore, he wagga hissa finger again and say, 'No smokin in dissa car. Musta go to smokin' car. So we go to smokin' car and I smoka my biga cigar."

"Then my beautiful Virginia and I, we go to sleeper car anda go to bed. We just about to go boomada boomada and the conductore, he walka through da hall shouting at da top of hissa voice, 'Nofolka Virginia! Nofolka Virginia!' Nexta time, Ima gonna takea da bus!"

BASIC MATH

A man left the following note for his wife:

My Dear Wife,

You will surely understand that I have certain needs that a woman of fifty-four years can no longer satisfy. I am very happy with you, and I value you as a good wife. Therefore, after reading this letter, I hope that you will not wrongly interpret the fact that I will be spending the evening with my eighteen year old secretary at the Comfort Inn Hotel. Please don't be perturbed. I shall be home before midnight.

When the man came home, he found the following letter on the dining room table:

My Dear Husband,

I received your letter and thank you for your honesty. I would like to take this opportunity to remind you that you are also

Liquor Up Front, Poker in the Rear

fifty-four years old. At the same time I would like to inform you that as you read this I will be at the Hotel Fiesta with Michael, my tennis coach, who like your secretary is eighteen years old. As a successful businessman with an excellent knowledge of mathematics you will understand that we are in the same situation - although with one small difference. Eighteen goes into fifty-four a <u>lot</u> more times than fifty-four goes into eighteen. Therefore, I will not be back until lunchtime tomorrow!

MEDICAL MIRACLE

An eighty-year-old man went to his doctor for his annual check-up. The doctor asked him how he was feeling, and the man said, "I've never felt better. I now have a twenty-year-old bride who is pregnant with my child. What do you think about that?"

The doctor considered his question for a minute and then began, "I have an older friend, much like you, who is an avid trophy hunter and never misses a season. One day when he was going out hunting he was in a bit of a hurry, and accidentally picked up his walking cane instead of his gun. When he got to the creek, he saw a prime beaver sitting beside the stream of water. He raised his cane and went, 'bang, bang.' Suddenly two shots rang out, and the beaver fell over dead. What do you think of that?"

The eighty-year-old said, "I'd say somebody else pumped a couple of rounds into that beaver.

The doctor replied, "My point exactly."

Liquor Up Front, Poker in the Rear

HARRY

A first-grade teacher, Ms. Brooks, was having trouble with one of her students. The teacher asked him, "Harry, what's your problem?"

Harry answered, "I'm too smart for the first grade. My sister is in the third grade, and I'm smarter than she is! I think I should be in the third grade too!"

Ms. Brooks had had enough, so she took Harry to the principal's office.

While Harry waited in the outer office, the teacher explained to the principal what the situation was. The principal told Ms. Brooks he would give the boy a test. If he failed to answer any of his questions he was to go back to the first grade and behave himself. She agreed.

Harry was brought in, the conditions were explained to him, and he agreed to take the test.

The principal asked, "What is three times

Liquor Up Front, Poker in the Rear

three?"

Harry answered, "Nine."

The principal asked, "What is six times six?"

Harry replied, "Thirty-six."

And so it went with every question the principal thought a third grader should know.

The principal looked at Ms. Brooks and told her, "I think Harry can go to the third grade."

Ms. Brooks said to the principal, "Let me ask him some questions."

The principal and Harry both agreed.

Ms. Brooks asked, "What does a cow have four of that I have only two of?"

After a moment Harry said, "Legs."

Ms. Brooks asked, "What do you have in your pants that I do not have?"

The principal wondered why would she ask such a question!

Harry replied, "Pockets."

Ms. Brooks asked, "What does a dog do, that a man steps into?"

Harry said, "Pants."

Liquor Up Front, Poker in the Rear

Ms. Brooks asked, "What starts with a C, ends with a T, is hairy, oval, delicious and contains thin, whitish liquid?"

Harry replied, "A coconut."

The principal sat forward with his mouth hanging open.

Ms. Brooks asked, "What goes in hard and pink, and comes out soft and sticky?"

The principal's eyes opened really wide, and before he could stop it the answer came.

Harry answered, "Bubble gum."

Ms. Brooks asked, "What does a man do standing up, a woman do sitting down, and a dog do on three legs?"

Harry said, "Shake hands."

The principal was trembling.

Ms. Brooks asked, "What word starts with an 'F,' ends in 'UCK,' and provides a lot of heat and excitement?"

Harry replied, "Firetruck."

The principal breathed a sigh of relief and told the teacher, "I want you to put Harry in the *fifth* grade. I got the last seven questions wrong......"

MY FIRST TIME

I recall my first time with a condom. I was sixteen or so, and went in to buy a package of them. There was a beautiful woman behind the counter, and she could see I was new at it.

She handed me the package, and asked if I knew how to wear one.

I honestly answered, "No"

So she unwrapped the package, took one out, and slipped it over her thumb. She cautioned me to make sure it was on tight and secure. I apparently still looked confused, so she looked all around the store. It was empty.

She said, "Just a minute," walked to the door, and locked it.

Taking my hand, she led me into the back room, unbuttoned her blouse, and removed it. She unhooked her bra and laid it aside. She asked, "Do these excite you?"

Well, I was so dumb-struck that all I

Liquor Up Front, Poker in the Rear

could do was nod my head.

She then said it was time to slip the condom on. As I did so she dropped her skirt, removed her panties, and lay down on a desk.

"Well, come on," she said, "We don't have much time." So I climbed on top of her.

It was so wonderful that, unfortunately, I couldn't hold back and POW, I was done within a few moments.

She looked at me with a frown. "Did you put that condom on first?"

I said, "I sure did." And I held up my thumb to show her!

HUMAN KINDNESS

A man was sitting on a beach who had tragically lost all of his arms and legs in a recent car accident.

During the long afternoon, as he remained on the beach, three women separately walked past him. Each felt very sorry for the poor man.

The first woman said, "Have you ever had a hug?"

The man said. "No," so she gave him a hug and walked on.

The second woman said, "Have you ever had a kiss?"

The man said, "No," so she gave him a kiss and walked on.

The third woman came to him and said, "Have you ever been fucked?"

The fellow swallowed hard and said, "No."

She said, "Well, you *will* be when the tide comes in!"

A GOOD DEAL

Two old friends were just about to tee off at the first hole of their local golf course when a chap carrying a golf bag called out to them, "Do you mind if join you? My partner didn't turn up."

"Sure," they said, "You're more than welcome."

So they started playing and enjoyed the game and the company of the newcomer.

Part way around the course one of the friends asked the newcomer, "What do you do for a living?"

"I'm a hit man," was the reply.

"You're joking!" was the response.

"No, I'm not," he said as he reached into his golf bag and pulled out a beautiful Martini sniper's rifle with a large telescopic sight. "Here are my tools."

"That's a beautiful telescopic sight," said the other friend, "Can I take a look? I think I might be able to see my house from here."

Liquor Up Front, Poker in the Rear

So he picked up the rifle and looked through the sight in the direction of his house.

"Yeah, I can see my house all right! This sight is fantastic. I can see right in the window."

"Wow, I can see my wife in the bedroom. Ha ha, I can see she's naked! What's that? Wait a minute, that's my neighbor in there with her... and he's naked too! That bitch!"

He turned to the hit man and asked, "How much do you charge for a hit?"

"I do a flat rate. For you, one thousand dollars every time I pull the trigger."

"Can you do two for me now?"

"Sure, what do you want?"

"First, shoot my wife. She's always been mouthy, so shoot her in the mouth. Then the neighbor. He's a friend of mine, a bit of a ladies man, so just shoot his dick off to teach him a lesson."

The hitman took the rifle and took aim, standing perfectly still for a few minutes.

"Are you going to do it or not?" said the man impatiently.

Liquor Up Front, Poker in the Rear

"Just wait a moment, be patient," said the hit man calmly, "I think I can save you a grand here....."

LADY GOLFER

Four lawyers in a law firm lived and died for their Saturday morning round of golf. It was their favorite moment of the week. Then one of the lawyers was transferred to an office in another city, and it wasn't quite the same without him.

A new woman lawyer soon joined their law firm, and one day she overheard the remaining three talking about their golf round at the coffee table.

Curious, she spoke up. "You know, I used to play on my golf team in college and was pretty good. Would you mind if I joined you next week?"

The three lawyers looked at each other. They were hesitant. Not one of them wanted to say 'yes,' but she had them on the spot. Finally one man said it would be okay, but added they would be starting pretty early - at six in the morning. He figured the early tee time would discourage her immediately.

Liquor Up Front, Poker in the Rear

The woman said this might be a problem, and asked if she could possibly be up to fifteen minutes late. They rolled their eyes, but said it would be okay. She smiled and said, "Good, then I'll be there either at six or six-fifteen."

She showed up right at six-fifteen and wound up beating all three of them with an eye-opening two-under par round. She was a fun and pleasant person the entire time, and the guys were impressed! Back in the clubhouse they congratulated her, and happily invited her back the following week.

She smiled and said, "Sure, I'll be here at six or six-fifteen."

The next week she showed up at six-o'clock sharp on Saturday morning. This time, she played left-handed. The three lawyers were incredulous, as she still managed to beat them with an even par round despite playing with her left-hand.

By now the guys were totally amazed, but wondered if she was just trying to make them look bad by beating them left-handed. They couldn't figure her out. She

Liquor Up Front, Poker in the Rear

was again very pleasant and didn't seem to be showing them up, but each man began to harbor a burning desire to beat her!

In the third week they all had their game faces on. But this week she was fifteen minutes late! This had the guys irritable because each was determined to play the best round of golf of his life to beat her. As they waited for her, they figured her late arrival was some petty gamesmanship on her part.

Finally she showed up. This week the lady lawyer played right-handed, which was a good thing since she narrowly beat all three of them. She was so gracious and so complimentary of their strong play, it was hard to keep a grudge against her. This woman was a riddle no one could figure out!

Back in the clubhouse she had all three guys shaking their heads at her ability. They had a couple beers after their round, which helped the conversation loosen up.

Finally one of the men could contain his curiosity no longer. He asked her point blank, "How do you decide if you're going

Liquor Up Front, Poker in the Rear

to golf right-handed or left-handed?"

The lady blushed and grinned. She said, "That's easy. When my dad taught me to play golf, I learned I was ambidextrous. I have always had fun switching back and forth. Then when I met my husband in college and got married, I discovered he always sleeps in the nude. From then on I developed a silly habit. Right before I left in the morning for golf practice I would pull the covers off him. If his penis was pointing to the right, I golfed right-handed. If it was pointed to the left, I golfed left-handed. All the girls on the team thought this was hysterical."

Astonished at this bizarre information, one of the guys shot back, "But what if it's pointed straight up in the air?"

"*Then...*" she winked, "I'm fifteen minutes late!"

Liquor Up Front, Poker in the Rear

BARBIE DOLL

A little girl was in line to see Santa, and when it was her turn she climbed up on his lap.

Santa asked, "What would you like Santa to bring you for Christmas?"

The little girl replied, "I want a Barbie, and a G.I. Joe."

Santa looked at the little girl for a moment and said, "I thought Barbie came with Ken?"

"No," said the little girl. "She comes with G.I. Joe. She *fakes* it with Ken!"

Liquor Up Front, Poker in the Rear

FINISHED?

A virile young Brazilian man was relaxing at his favorite bar in Rio when he managed to attract a spectacular young blonde. Things progressed to the point where he invited her back to his apartment, and after some small talk they retired to his bedroom for doing what comes naturally.

After a pleasant interlude he asked with a smile, "So... you finish?"

She paused for a second, frowned, and replied, "No."

Surprised, the young man reached for her and the love-making resumed. This time she thrashed about wildly and there were screams of passion.

The love-making ended, and again the young man smiled and asked, "You finish?"

Again, after a short pause, she returned his smile, cuddled closer to him, and softly said, "No."

Liquor Up Front, Poker in the Rear

Stunned, but damned if this woman was going to outlast him, the young man reached for her again. Using the last of his strength he barely managed it, but they climaxed simultaneously - wildly screaming, bucking, clawing and twisting the bed sheets.

The exhausted young man fell onto his back, gasping. Barely able to turn his head, he looked into her eyes, smiled proudly, and asked again, "You finish?"

Barely able to speak, she whispered in his ear, "No....... I'm Norwegian!"

SPERM COUNT

An old man went to his doctor to get a sperm count.

The doctor gave the man a jar and said, "Take this jar home and bring me back a semen sample tomorrow."

The next day the old man returned to the doctor's office and gave him the jar, which was as clean and empty as on the previous day.

The doctor asked what happened, and the man explained, "Well, doc, it's like this..... First I tried with my right hand, but nothing. Then I tried with my left hand, but still nothing. Then I asked my wife for help. She tried with her right hand, then her left, still nothing. She even tried with her mouth, first with the teeth in, then with her teeth out, and still nothing. We even called up Arlene, the lady next door, and she tried too, first with both hands, then an armpit, and she even tried squeez'n it between her knees, but still

Liquor Up Front, Poker in the Rear

nothing."

The doctor was shocked! "You asked your neighbor?"

The old Man replied, "Yep, but no matter what all of us tried, with our arthritis, we *still* couldn't get the damn jar open!"

THE PEACHES

An old farmer was selling his peaches door to door. He knocked on a door, and a very pretty young lady dressed in an extremely sheer negligee answered.

He raised his basket to show her the peaches and asked, "Would you like to buy some peaches?"

She pulled the top of the negligee to one side, showing her breast, and asked, "Are they as firm as this?"

He nodded his head and said, "Yes," and a little tear ran from his eye.

Then she pulled the other side of her negligee off while asking, "Are they nice and pink like this?"

The farmer said, "Yes," and another tear came from the other eye.

Then lady then lifted the bottom of her negligee and asked, "And are they as fuzzy as this?"

He again said, "Yes!" and broke down

Liquor Up Front, Poker in the Rear

crying.

The lady said "What in the world is wrong with you? Why are you crying?"

Drying his eyes he said, "The drought got my corn, the flood got my cotton, and now I'm gonna get screwed out of my *peaches!*"

Liquor Up Front, Poker in the Rear

THE DILDO

A little old lady, well into her eighties, slowly entered the front door of a sex shop. Obviously very unstable on her feet, she wobbled as she crossed the store to the register.

Finally arriving at the counter, and grabbing it for support, she slowly asked the sales clerk, "Dddooo youuuu hhhave dddddiilllldosss?"

The clerk, politely trying not to burst out laughing, replied, "Yes we do have dildos. Actually, we carry many different models."

The old woman then asked, "Dddddoooo yyyouuuu ccaarrryy aaa pppinkk onnee, tttenn inchessss lllong aaandd aabboutt ttwoo inchesss ththiickk...... aaaaaand rrrrrunns by bbaatteries?"

The clerk responded, "Yes, we do!"

"Dddddddddooooooo yyyyyoooouuuu kknnnoooww hhhoww tttoo tttturrrnnn tttttthe ssunoooffabbitch offffff???"

Liquor Up Front, Poker in the Rear

DRUG RESEARCH

In pharmacology, all drugs have two names - a trade name and a generic name. For example, the trade name of Tylenol is acetaminophen. Aleve is known as naproxen, and Advil is ibuprofen. The industry has been looking for a generic name for Viagra. After consideration by a team of government experts, it recently announced the generic name of 'mycoxafloppin.' Also considered were 'mycoxafailin,' 'mydixadrupin,' 'dixafix,' 'mydixarin,' 'mydixadud,' and of course, 'ibepokin.'

Pfizer Inc. recently indicated that Viagra will soon be available in liquid form and be marketed by Pepsi Cola as a power beverage suitable for use as a mixer. Pepsi's ad campaign claims it will now be possible for a man to literally pour himself a stiff one. Obviously, they can no longer call this a 'soft drink.' This additive gives a new

Liquor Up Front, Poker in the Rear

meaning to the names of cocktails, highballs and just a good old fashioned stiff drink. Pepsi will market the new concoction by the name of 'Mount & Do.'

It should also be noted that over the past few years more money has been spent on breast implants and Viagra than on Alzheimer's research. It is believed that as the population ages, there will be a large number of people wandering around with huge breasts and giant erections who can't seem to remember what to do with them!

Liquor Up Front, Poker in the Rear

DEVIL OF A DEAL

One day in the future Jesse Jackson has a heart attack and dies. He immediately goes to hell, where the devil is waiting for him.

"I don't know what to do here," says the devil. "You are on my list, but I have no room for you. You definitely have to stay here, so I'll tell you what I'm going to do. I've got a couple of folks here who weren't quite as bad as you. I'll let one of them go, but you have to take their place. I'll even let YOU decide who leaves. You'll be taking their place of course."

Jesse thought that sounded pretty good, so the devil opened the door to the first room. In it was Ted Kennedy and a large pool of water. He kept diving in, and surfacing empty handed. Over, and over, and over, he dove in and surfaced with nothing. Such was his fate in hell.

"No," Jesse said. "I don't think so. I'm not a good swimmer, and I don't think I

Liquor Up Front, Poker in the Rear

could do that all day long."

The devil led him to the door of the next room. In it was John Kerry with a sledgehammer and a room full of rocks. All he did was swing that hammer, time after time after time.

"No, I've got this problem with my shoulder. I would be in constant agony if all I could do was break rocks all day," commented Jesse.

The devil opened a third door. Through it Jesse saw Bill Clinton, lying on the floor with his arms tied over his head and his legs restrained in a spread-eagle pose. Bent over him was Monica Lewinsky, and she was giving him a blow job.

Jesse looked at this in shocked disbelief, and finally said, "Yeah, I can handle this!"

The devil smiled and said... "Okay Monica, you're free to go!"

Liquor Up Front, Poker in the Rear

HAPPY BIRTHDAY

A young man wanted to purchase a gift for his new sweetheart's birthday, and as they had not been dating very long, and after careful consideration, he decided that a pair of gloves would strike the right note - romantic, but not too personal.

Accompanied by his sweetheart's younger sister, he went to Nordstrom and bought a pair of white gloves.

While they were there the sister purchased a pair of panties for herself. During the wrapping, the clerk mixed up the items and the sister got the gloves and the sweetheart got the panties. Without checking the contents, the young man sealed the package and sent it to his sweetheart with the following note:

"I chose these because I noticed that you are not in the habit of wearing any when we go out in the evening. If it had not been for

Liquor Up Front, Poker in the Rear

your sister, I would have chosen the long ones with the buttons, but she wears short ones that are easier to remove.

These are a delicate shade, but the lady I bought them from showed me the pair she had been wearing for the past three weeks and they were hardly soiled. I had her try yours on for me and she looked really smart. I wish I was there to put them on you for you the first time, as no doubt other hands will come in contact with them before I have a chance to see you again.

When you take them off, remember to blow in them before putting them away as they will naturally be a little damp from wearing. Just think how many times I will kiss them during the coming year. I hope you will wear them for me on Friday night.

P.S.- The latest style is to wear them folded down with a little fur showing!"

CHEAP DIAGNOSIS

One day Pete complained to his friend, "My elbow really hurts. I guess I should see a doctor."

His friend said, "Don't do that. There's a computer at the drug store that can diagnose anything quicker and cheaper than a doctor. Put in a sample of your urine, and the computer will diagnose your problem and tell you what to do. It only costs ten dollars."

Pete figured he had nothing to lose, so he filled a jar with a urine sample and went to the drug store. Finding the computer, he poured in the sample and deposited the money.

The computer started making some noise and lights started flashing. After a brief pause, out popped a small slip of paper which read:

You have tennis elbow. Soak your arm in

Liquor Up Front, Poker in the Rear

warm water, and avoid heavy labor. It will be better in two weeks.

That evening, while thinking how amazing this new technology was and how it would change medical science forever, he began to wonder if it could be fooled. He decided to give it a try. He mixed together some tap water, a stool sample from his dog, and urine samples from his wife and daughter. To top it off, he masturbated into the concoction. He went back to the drug store, located the computer, poured in the sample and deposited ten dollars.

The machine again made the usual noises, flashed its lights, and printed out the following analysis:

Your tap water is too hard. Get a water softener.

Your dog has ringworm. Bathe him with anti-fungal shampoo.

Your daughter is using cocaine. Put her in a rehabilitation clinic.

Liquor Up Front, Poker in the Rear

Your wife is pregnant . . . twin girls. They aren't yours. Get a lawyer.

And if you don't stop jerking off, your elbow will <u>never</u> get better!

Liquor Up Front, Poker in the Rear

LITTLE GENIE

Two friends were in a bar drinking a beer when one pulled out a cigar. He didn't have a lighter, so he asked his friend if he had one.

"I sure do," he replied as he reached into his pocket and pulled out a ten-inch Bic lighter.

"Wow!" he exclaimed, "where did you get that monster?"

"I got it from my genie."

"You have a genie?" he asked.

"Yes, he's right here in my pocket."

"Could I see him?"

The friend then reached into his pocket and pulled out a very small genie.

The man said, "I'm a good friend of your master. Will you grant me one wish?"

"Yes I will," the genie said, so the man asked him for a million bucks. The genie then hopped back into his master's pocket and left the man standing there waiting for

Liquor Up Front, Poker in the Rear

his money.

About that time a duck walked into the bar, followed by another. Then more ducks came pouring in. Before long the entire bar had ducks everywhere. The man looked at his buddy, "What is going on here? I asked for a million *bucks*, not ducks!"

His friend answered, "I forgot to tell you, the genie is hard of hearing. Do you really think I asked him for a ten-inch *Bic?*"

Liquor Up Front, Poker in the Rear

A FAIRY TALE

Cinderella wanted to go to the ball, but her wicked stepmother wouldn't let her. As she sat crying in the garden, her fairy godmother appeared and promised to provide Cinderella with everything she needed to go to the ball - but only on two conditions.

"First, you must wear a diaphragm."

Cinderella agreed.

"Second, you must be home by two AM. Any later, and your diaphragm will turn into a pumpkin."

Cinderella agreed, but when the appointed hour came she didn't show up.

Finally at five AM Cinderella arrived, looking love struck and very satisfied.

"Where have you been?" demanded the Fairy Godmother. "Your diaphragm was supposed to turn into a pumpkin three hours ago!!!"

"I met a prince, Fairy Godmother. He

Liquor Up Front, Poker in the Rear

took care of everything."

The Fairy Godmother stated, "I know of no prince with that kind of power! Tell me his name!"

Cinderella replied, "I can't remember, exactly. Peter, Peter, something or other..."

Liquor Up Front, Poker in the Rear

AMAZING CLAUDE

It was opening night at the Orpheum and *The Amazing Claude* was topping the bill. Hundreds of people came from miles around to see the famed hypnotist do his stuff. As Claude took to the stage he announced, "Unlike most stage hypnotists who invite two or three people up onto the stage to be put into a trance, I intend to hypnotize each and every member of this audience."

The excitement was almost electric as Claude withdrew a beautiful antique pocket watch from his coat. "I want you each to keep your eye on this antique watch. It's a very *special* watch. It's been in my family for six generations."

He began to swing the watch gently back and forth while quietly chanting, "Watch the watch, watch the watch, watch the watch..."

The crowd became mesmerized as the watch swayed back and forth, light gleaming off its polished surface. Hundreds of pairs of

Liquor Up Front, Poker in the Rear

eyes followed the swaying watch until suddenly it slipped from the hypnotist's fingers and fell to the floor, breaking into a hundred pieces.

"FUCK!" shouted the hypnotist.

It took three weeks to clean up the theater...

HAPPY ANNIVERSARY

Three guys were sitting in a bar talking. One was a doctor, one was a lawyer, and one was a biker. After a sip of his martini, the doctor said, "You know, tomorrow is my anniversary. I got my wife a diamond ring and a new Mercedes. I figure that if she doesn't like the diamond ring she will at least like the Mercedes, and she will know that I love her."

After finishing his scotch, the lawyer replied, "Well, on my last anniversary I got my wife a string of pearls and a trip to the Bahamas. I figured that if she didn't like the pearls she would at least like the trip, and she would know that I love her."

The biker then took a big swig from his beer and said, "Yeah? Well, for my anniversary I got my old lady a T-shirt and a vibrator. I figured that if she didn't like the T-shirt… she could go fuck herself!"

Liquor Up Front, Poker in the Rear

IT'S THE THOUGHT

Joe was talking to his buddy at the bar and he said, "I don't know what to get my wife for her birthday - she has everything, and besides, she can afford to buy anything she wants, so I'm stumped."

His buddy said, "I have an idea - why don't you make up a certificate saying she can have sixty minutes of great sex, *any* way she wants it – she'll probably be thrilled!"

So that's what Joe did.

The next day at the bar his buddy approached him and asked, "Well? Did you take my suggestion?"

"Yes, I did," said Joe.

"Did she like it?" His buddy prodded.

"Oh yes! She jumped up, thanked me, kissed me on the forehead, and ran out the door yelling, "I'll be back in an hour!"

THE EULOGY

A woman got married, and had eleven children. Then her husband died. She married again, and had five more children. Again, her husband died. She remarried yet again, and this time had three more children. Again, her husband died. And alas, she herself finally died.

Standing before her coffin, the preacher prayed for her. He thanked the Lord for this very loving woman and said, "Lord, they're finally together."

One mourner leaned over and quietly asked her friend, "Do you think he means her first, second or third husband?"

The friend replied, "I think he means her *legs*."

Liquor Up Front, Poker in the Rear

THREE VIRGINS

A mother had three virgin daughters, all of whom were getting married within a short time period. Because Mom was a bit worried about how their sex lives would get started, she made them all promise to send a postcard from their honeymoons with a few words about how marital sex felt.

The first girl sent a card from Hawaii two days after the wedding. The card said nothing but 'Nescafe.' Mom was puzzled at first, but then went the kitchen and got out the Nescafe jar. It said, *Good to the Last Drop.*

Mom blushed, but was pleased for her daughter.

The second girl sent a card from Vermont a week after her wedding which read, 'Benson & Hedges.' Mom now knew to go straight to her husband's cigarettes, and she read from the Benson & Hedges pack, *Extra Long. King Size.*

Liquor Up Front, Poker in the Rear

She was again slightly embarrassed, but still happy for her daughter.

The third girl left for her honeymoon in the Caribbean. Mom waited for a week, but received nothing. Another week went by, and still nothing. Then, after a whole month, a card finally arrived. Written on it with shaky handwriting were the words 'British Airways.' Mom took out her latest *Harper's Bazaar* magazine, flipped through the pages fearing the worst, and finally found the ad for British Airways.

The ad said, *Three times a day, seven days a week, both ways!*

The mother fainted.

Liquor Up Front, Poker in the Rear

JOLT OF CAFFEINE

An elderly woman went to a doctor and asked his help to revive her husband's sex drive.

"What about trying Viagra?" asked the doctor.

"Not a chance," said Mrs. Murphy. "He won't even take an aspirin for a headache."

"No problem," replied the doctor. "Drop it into his coffee, and he won't even taste it. Try it, and come back in a week to let me know how you got on."

A week later Mrs. Murphy returned to the doctor and he inquired as to how things had gone.

"Oh it was terrible, just terrible, doctor!"

"What happened?" asks the doctor.

"Well I did as you advised and slipped it in his coffee. The effect was immediate. He jumped straight up, swept the cutlery off the table, at the same time ripping my clothes off, and then proceeded to make passionate

Liquor Up Front, Poker in the Rear

love to me on the tabletop. It was terrible."

"What was terrible?" asked the doctor. "Was the sex not good?"

"Oh no doctor, the sex was the best I've had in twenty-five years, but I'll never be able to show my face in McDonald's again!"

Liquor Up Front, Poker in the Rear

CHOO CHOO!

A mother was working in the kitchen, listening to her five-year-old son playing with his new electric train in the living room. She heard the train stop and her son saying, "All of you bastards who want off, get the hell off now, 'cause we are runnin' late! And all of you bastards who are getting on, get your ass in the train, 'cause we're going down the tracks real soon."

The horrified mother went in and told her son, "We don't use that kind of language in this house. Now I want you to go to your room and stay there for two hours. When you come out you may play with your train, but I want you to use nice language."

Two hours later the son came out of his bedroom and resumed playing with his train. Soon the train stopped, and the mother heard her son say, "Attention please. All passengers who are disembarking the train, please remember to take all of your

Liquor Up Front, Poker in the Rear

belongings with you. We thank you for travelling with us today." And she heard the little boy continue, "For those of you just boarding, we ask you to store all of your hand luggage under your seat. Remember, there is no smoking on the train. We hope you will have a pleasant and relaxing journey with us today."

As the mother began to smile the child added, "For those of you who are pissed off about the fucking TWO HOUR delay, please direct your complaints to the fat bitch in the kitchen!"

FILL 'ER UP

There was a gas station in redneck country trying to increase sales, so the owner put up a sign which said *Free Sex With Fill-up.*

Soon a redneck customer pulled in, filled his tank, and asked for his free sex. The owner told him to pick a number from one to ten, and if he guessed correctly he would get his free sex. The buyer guessed eight - and the proprietor said, "No, but you were close. The number was seven. Sorry, no free sex, but maybe next time."

Some time thereafter the same man, along with his buddy this time, pulled in again for a fill-up and again he asked for his free sex. The proprietor gave him the same story and asked him to guess the correct number. The man guessed two this time, and the proprietor said, "Sorry, it was three. You were close, but no free sex this time."

As they were driving away the driver said

Liquor Up Front, Poker in the Rear

to his buddy, "I think that game is rigged. He doesn't give away free sex."

The buddy replied, "No, it ain't rigged. My wife won *twice* last week!"

SAFE SMOKES

Two elderly ladies were outside their nursing home having a smoke when it started to rain. One of the ladies pulled out a condom, cut off the end, put it over her cigarette, and continued smoking.

The other lady asked, "What's that?"

"A condom," she responded. "This way my cigarette doesn't get wet."

"Where did you get it?" the other lady asked.

"You can get them at any drugstore."

The next day the first lady hobbled herself down to the local drugstore and announced to the pharmacist that she wanted a box of condoms. The guy looked at her kind of strangely (she was, after all, over eighty years of age), but politely asked what brand she preferred.

"It doesn't matter," she replied, "as long as it fits on a Camel!"

Liquor Up Front, Poker in the Rear

FIVE SECRETS
TO A PERFECT RELATIONSHIP

1. It's important to have a lover who helps out at home, cooks, cleans up, and has a job.

2. It's important to have a lover who can make you laugh.

3. It's important to have a lover you can trust and who doesn't lie to you.

4. It's important to have a lover who is good in bed, and who likes to be with you.

5. It's very, *very* important that these four people don't know each other!

Liquor Up Front, Poker in the Rear

THE AMAZING TEXAN

A traveling salesman visited a small town in the Midwest and saw a circus banner reading *Don't Miss the Amazing Texan.*

Curious, he bought a ticket. The tent went dark. Suddenly trumpets blared and all eyes turned to the center ring. There, spotlit in the center ring, was a table with three walnuts on it. Standing next to it was an old retired cowboy.

Suddenly the old man unzipped his pants, whipped out a huge penis, and smashed all three walnuts with three mighty swings!

The audience erupted in applause, and the elderly Texan was carried off on the shoulders of the crowd.

Ten years later the salesman visited the same little town and he saws a faded sign for the same circus and the same event... *Don't Miss the Amazing Texan.*

He couldn't believe the old guy was still alive, much less still doing his act - so he

Liquor Up Front, Poker in the Rear

bought a ticket.

Again, the center ring was illuminated. This time, instead of walnuts, three coconuts were placed on the table. The Texan stood before them, then suddenly unzipped his fly and smashed the coconuts with three swings of his amazing member.

The crowd went absolutely wild! Flabbergasted, the salesman requested a meeting with him after the show.

"You're incredible," he told the Texan. "But there's something I just have to know. You're older now, so why the switch from walnuts to coconuts?"

"Well," said the Texan, "my *eyes* just ain't what they used to be!"

Liquor Up Front, Poker in the Rear

CATHOUSE PARROT

A woman went to a pet shop and immediately spotted a large, beautiful parrot. There was a sign on the cage that said the price was fifty dollars.

"Why so little," she asked the pet store owner.

The owner looked at her sheepishly and said, "Look, I should tell you first that for years this bird lived in a house of prostitution, and sometimes it says some pretty vulgar stuff."

The woman thought about this, but decided she had to have the bird anyway. She took it home, hung the bird's cage up in her living room, and waited for it to say something.

The bird looked around the room, then at her, and said, "New house, new madam."

The woman was a bit shocked at the implication, but then thought, "That's really not so bad."

Liquor Up Front, Poker in the Rear

When her two teenage daughters returned from school the bird saw them and said, "New house, new madam, new girls."

The girls and the woman were a bit offended, but then began to laugh about the situation, considering how and where the parrot had been raised.

Moments later the woman's husband came home from work. The bird looked at him and said, "Hi, Frank!"

Liquor Up Front, Poker in the Rear

LEARNING TO CUSS

A six-year-old and a four-year-old were upstairs in their bedroom.

"You know what?" said the six-year-old. "I think it's about time we started cussing."

The four-year-old nodded his head in agreement.

The six-year-old continued, "When we go downstairs for breakfast I'm gonna say something with 'hell,' and you say something with 'ass.'"

The four-year-old agreed enthusiastically. When the mother walked into the kitchen and asked the six-year-old what he wanted for breakfast, he replied, "Aw, hell, Mom, I guess I'll have some Cheerios."

WHACK! He flew out of his chair, tumbled across the kitchen floor, got up, and ran upstairs crying his eyes out - with his mother in hot pursuit, slapping his rear every step of the way.

His mom locked him in his room and

Liquor Up Front, Poker in the Rear

shouted, "You can stay there until I let you out!"

She then came back downstairs, looked at the four-year-old, and asked with a stern voice, "And what do YOU want for breakfast, young man?"

"I don't know," he blubbered, "but you can bet your ass it won't be *Cheerios!*"

Liquor Up Front, Poker in the Rear

MISS MANNERS

A teacher trying to teach good manners asked a student, "Michael, if you were on a date, and having supper with a nice young lady, how would you tell her that you have to go to the bathroom?"

"Just a minute, I have to go piss."

The teacher replied, "That would be rude and impolite! What about you, John, how would you say it?"

"I am sorry, but I really need to go to the bathroom. I'll be right back."

The teacher responded, "That's better, but it's still not very nice to say the word bathroom at the table. How about you Peter, are you able to use your intelligence for once and show us your good manners?"

"I'd say 'Darling, may I be excused for a moment, I have to go shake hands with a very dear friend of mine, whom I hope you'll get to meet after supper.'"

The teacher fainted.

Liquor Up Front, Poker in the Rear

REMEMBER ME?

A man who was standing in line at a checkout counter of a grocery store was surprised when a very attractive woman behind him said, "Hello!" Her face was beaming.

He gave her that 'who are you?' look, and couldn't remember ever having seen her before.

Then, noticing his look, she figured she had made a mistake and apologized. "Look," she said, "I'm really sorry, but when I first saw you I thought you were the father of one of my children." She then walked out of the store.

The guy was dumbfounded and thought to himself, "What the hell is this world coming to? Here is an attractive woman who can't even keep track of who fathers her children!"

Then he got a little panicky. "I don't remember her," he thought, "but MAYBE....

Liquor Up Front, Poker in the Rear

during one of the wild parties he had been to when he was in college, perhaps he did father her child!"

He ran from the store and caught her in the parking lot and asked, "Are you the girl I met at a party in college, and then we got really drunk and had wild crazy sex on the pool table in front of everyone?"

"No," she said with a horrified look on her face. "I'm your son's second grade teacher!"

TEENAGE SEX

The mother of a seventeen-year-old girl was concerned that her daughter was having sex. She was worried the girl might become pregnant and adversely impact the family's status, so she consulted the family doctor.

The doctor told her that teenagers today were very willful, and any attempt to stop the girl would probably result in rebellion. He then told her to arrange for her daughter to be put on birth control, and until then talk to her and give her a box of condoms.

Later that evening, as her daughter was preparing for a date, the woman told her about the situation and handed her a box of condoms. The girl burst out laughing and reached over to hug her mother saying, "Oh Mom! You don't have to worry about *that!* I'm dating Susan!"

THE "F" WORD

There are only ten times in all of history where the "F" word has been considered acceptable for use. They are as follows:

10. "What the fuck was *that?*"
-- Mayor of Hiroshima, 1945

9. "Where did all those fucking Indians come from?"
-- George Armstrong Custer, 1877

8. "Any fucking moronic idiot could understand that!"
-- Albert Einstein, 1938

7. "It does fucking so look like her!"
-- Pablo Picasso, 1926

6. "How the fuck did you work *that* out?"
-- Pythagoras, 126 BC

5. "You want WHAT on the fucking ceiling?"
-- Michelangelo, 1566

Liquor Up Front, Poker in the Rear

4. "Where in the fuck *are* we?"
   -- Amelia Earhart, 1937

3. "Scattered showers, my fucking ass!"
   -- Noah, 4314 BC

2. "C'mon, Monica. Who the fuck is going to find out?"
   – William Jefferson Clinton, 1998

1. "Geez, I didn't think they'd get *this* fucking pissed!"
   -- Saddam Hussein, 2003

Liquor Up Front, Poker in the Rear

LOGICAL DEDUCTION

A woman was shopping at her local supermarket where she selected the following items:

> *A half-gallon of 2% milk,*
> *A carton of eggs,*
> *A quart of orange juice,*
> *A head of romaine lettuce,*
> *A 2 lb. can of coffee,*
> *A 1 lb package of bacon.*

As she was loading her items onto the conveyor belt to check out, a drunk standing behind her watched as she placed the items in front of the cashier.

While the cashier was ringing up her purchase the drunk calmly stated, "You must be single."

The woman was a bit startled by this proclamation, but she was intrigued by the derelict's intuition, since she *was* indeed

Liquor Up Front, Poker in the Rear

single.

She looked at her six items on the belt and saw nothing particularly unusual about her selections which could have tipped off the drunk to her marital status.

With her curiosity getting the better of her, she finally said "Well, you know what, you are absolutely correct. But, how on earth did you know that?"

The drunk replied, "Because you're uglier 'n shit!"

Liquor Up Front, Poker in the Rear

TRAFFIC STOP

An elderly couple was driving cross-country when the wife got pulled over.

The officer said, "Ma'am, did you know you were speeding?"

The woman turned to her husband and asked, "What did he say?"

The old man yelled, "He said you were speeding."

The patrolman said, "May I see your license?"

The woman asked her husband, "What did he say?"

The old man yelled, "He wants to see your license."

The woman gave him her license.

The patrolman said, "I see you are from Arkansas. I spent some time there once. Had the worst sex with a woman I ever had..."

The woman asked her husband, "What did he say?"

"HE THINKS HE KNOWS YOU!"

Liquor Up Front, Poker in the Rear

DIVORCE LETTER

Dear Connie,

I know the counselor said we shouldn't contact each other during our "cooling off" period, but I couldn't wait anymore. The day you left, I swore I'd never talk to you again. But that was just the wounded little boy in me talking. Still, I never wanted to be the first one to make contact. In my fantasies, it was always you who would come crawling back to me. I guess my pride needed that. But now I see that my pride has cost me a lot of things. I'm tired of pretending I don't miss you. I don't care about looking bad anymore, or who makes the first move as long as one of us does.

Maybe it's time we let our hearts speak as loudly as our hurt. And this is what my heart says: "There's no one like you, Connie." I look for you in the eyes and breasts of every woman I see, but they're not you. They're

Liquor Up Front, Poker in the Rear

not even close. Two weeks ago I met this girl at Flamingos, and brought her home with me. I don't say this to hurt you, but just to illustrate the depth of my desperation.

She was young, maybe nineteen, with one of those perfect bodies that only youth and maybe a childhood spent ice skating can give you. I mean, just a perfect body. Tits like you wouldn't believe, and an ass that just wouldn't quit. It's every man's dream, right? But as I sat on the couch being blown by this stunner, I thought, 'look at the stuff we've made important in our lives.' It's all so superficial.

What does a perfect body mean? Does it make her better in bed? Well, in this case, yes, but you see what I'm getting at. Does it make her a better person? Does she have a better heart than my moderately attractive Connie? I doubt it. And I'd never really thought of that before.

I don't know, maybe I'm just growing up a little. Later, after I'd tossed her about a half a pint of throat yogurt, I found myself thinking, "Why do I feel so drained and

Liquor Up Front, Poker in the Rear

empty?" It wasn't just her flawless deep throat technique, or her slutty, shameless hunger, but something else. Some nagging feeling of loss. Why did it all feel so incomplete? And then it hit me. It didn't feel the same because you weren't there to watch. Do you know what I mean? Nothing feels the same without you. Jesus, Connie, I'm just going crazy without you. And everything I do just reminds me of you.

Do you remember Carol, that single mom we met at the Holiday Inn lounge last year? Well, she dropped by last week with a pan of lasagna. She said she figured I wasn't eating right without a woman around. I didn't know what she meant till later, but that's not the real story. Anyway, we had a few glasses of wine and the next thing you know, we're banging away in our old bedroom. And this tart was a total monster in the sack. She's giving me everything, you know, like a real woman does when she's not hung up about her weight or her career and whether the kids can hear us. And all of a sudden, she spots that tilting mirror on your

Liquor Up Front, Poker in the Rear

grandmother's old vanity. So she puts it on the floor and we straddle it, right, so we can watch ourselves. And it's totally hot, but it makes me sad, too. 'Cause I can't help thinking, "Why didn't Connie ever put the mirror on the floor? We've had this old vanity for what, fourteen years, and never used it as a sex toy."

Saturday, your sister dropped by with my copy of the restraining order. I mean, Vicky's just a kid and all, but she's got a pretty good head on her shoulders and she's been a real friend to me during this painful time. She's given me lots of good advice about you, and about women in general. She's pulling for us to get back together Connie, she really is. So we're doing Jell-O shots in a hot bubble bath and talking about happier times. Here's this teenage girl with the same DNA as you, and all I can do is think of how much she looks like you when you were eighteen. And that just about makes me cry.

And then it turns out Vicky's really into the whole anal thing, and that gets me to

Liquor Up Front, Poker in the Rear

thinking about how many times I pressured you about trying it and how that probably fueled some of the bitterness between us. But do you see how even then, when I'm thrusting inside your baby sister's cinnamon ring, all I can do is think of you? It's true, Connie. In your heart you must know it. Don't you think we could start over? Just wipe out all the grievances away and start fresh? I think we can.

If you feel the same please, please let me know. Otherwise, can you let me know where the fucking remote is?

All My Love,
Dan

Liquor Up Front, Poker in the Rear

FRANK FELDMAN

A man walked out to the street and caught a taxi cab just going by. He got into the taxi and the cabbie said, "Perfect timing. You're just like Frank."

The passenger said, "Who?"

The cabbie responded, "Frank Feldman. He's a guy who did everything right all the time. Like my coming along when you needed a cab, things happened like that to Frank Feldman every single time."

The passenger said, "There are always a few clouds over everybody."

The cabbie disagreed. "Nope, not Frank Feldman. He was a terrific athlete. He could have won the Grand Slam at tennis. He could golf with the pros. He sang like an opera baritone, danced like a Broadway star, and you should have heard him play the piano. He was an amazing guy."

The passenger said, "Sounds like he was something really special."

Liquor Up Front, Poker in the Rear

The cabbie added, "There's more! He had a memory like a computer. He remembered everybody's birthday. He knew all about wine, which foods to order, and which fork to eat them with. He could fix anything. Not like me. I change a fuse, and the whole street blacks out. But Frank Feldman, he could do *everything* right."

"Wow, some guy then..."

The cabbie continued, "He always knew the quickest way to go in traffic, and avoided traffic jams. Not like me. I always seem to get stuck in them. But Frank, he *never* made a mistake ... and he really knew how to treat a woman and make her feel good. He would never answer her back, even if she was in the wrong... and his clothing was always immaculate. Shoes highly polished too. He was the perfect man! He never made a mistake. No one could *ever* measure up to Frank Feldman."

The passenger nodded. "A truly amazing fellow! How did you meet him?"

"Well, I never actually *met* Frank. He died, and I'm married to his damn widow!"

Liquor Up Front, Poker in the Rear

TEE'D OFF

Harold had a week off so he decided to play golf every day, and early on Monday morning found himself paired with an attractive woman named Annette who turned out to be a very good golfer.

They started with a few casual bets, but by the time they reached the back nine it was a full-blown competition.

On the eighteenth green, Annette sank a long birdie putt for the win.

Harold congratulated her, and paid off his losses.

Annette asked for a ride home, and on the way told him, "You know Harold, I haven't enjoyed myself that much on the golf course in a long time. In fact, pull over so I can express my appreciation."

He did, they kissed, one thing led to another, and eventually she gave him the best blowjob he'd ever had.

The next morning they met on the first tee

Liquor Up Front, Poker in the Rear

and played together again. They had another magnificent day, enjoying each other's company and playing tight, competitive golf.

Again Annette beat him, but she once again showed her appreciation on the drive home with an amazing blowjob.

This went on all week, with Harold narrowly losing every day, his male ego bruised, but not unhappy.

On Friday's drive home Harold said, "Annette, you've been great to be with all this week, and tonight I'd like to return the favor. I made reservations at the best restaurant in town for us, and reserved the penthouse suite at the best hotel. What do you say?"

Annette burst into tears. "I can't!"

"What? Why not?" he asked.

"Because…" she sobbed, "I'm in the middle of a sex change, and the doctor hasn't completed that part of me yet!"

"What?" Aghast, Harold swerved off the road, screeched to a stop and cursed madly, overcome with emotion.

Liquor Up Front, Poker in the Rear

"I'm so sorry," said Annette, "You have a right to be angry with me."

"You bastard!" Harold screamed, his face bright red. "You cheating bastard! All week long you've been playing off the women's tees!"

Liquor Up Front, Poker in the Rear

OLD COWBOY

An old cowboy sat down at the Starbucks counter and ordered a cup of coffee. As he sat sipping it, a young woman sat down next to him.

She turned to the cowboy and asked, "Are you a real cowboy?"

He replied, "Well, I've spent my whole life breaking colts, working cows, going to rodeos, fixing fences, pulling calves, bailing hay, doctoring calves, cleaning my barn, fixing flats, working on tractors, and feeding my dogs… so I guess I'm a cowboy."

She said, "I'm a lesbian. I spend my whole day thinking about naked women. As soon as I get up in the morning, I think about naked women. When I shower, I think about naked women. When I watch television, I think about naked women. It seems like *everything* makes me think of naked women."

The two sat sipping in silence.

Liquor Up Front, Poker in the Rear

A little while later, a man sat down on the other side of the old cowboy and asked, Say are you a real cowboy?"

He replied, "I always *thought* I was, but I just found out I'm really a lesbian!"

THE FISHING TRIP

Dave's buddies were planning a big fishing trip, but he had to tell them he couldn't go this time because his wife wouldn't let him. After a lot of teasing and name calling Dave headed home, frustrated.

The following week Dave's buddies arrived at the lake to set up camp and were shocked to see Dave. He was already there with a cold beer, swag rolled out, fishing rod in hand, and a camp fire glowing.

"How did you talk your missus into letting you go, Dave?"

"I didn't have to," he replied. "Last week when I left I went home and sat in my chair with a beer to drown my sorrows. My wife snuck up behind me, covered my eyes, and said, 'Surprise!' When I peeled her hands back she was in a see through negligee and said, 'Carry me to the bedroom, tie me to the bed, and do whatever you want'… SO HERE I AM!"

Liquor Up Front, Poker in the Rear

ALL THAT GLITTERS

A woman went to her doctor's office to discuss a strange development. She has discovered a green spot on the inside of each thigh. They wouldn't wash off, they wouldn't scrape off, and they seemed to be getting worse. The doctor assured her that he'd get to the bottom of the problem, and told her not to worry until he got the tests back.

A few days later the woman's phone rang. Much to her relief, it was the doctor. She immediately begged to know what was causing the spots.

The doctor said, "You're perfectly healthy, and there's no problem. But I'm wondering... was your boyfriend that Harley guy out in the waiting room?"

The woman stammered, "Why, yes... but how did you know?"

"Tell him his earrings aren't *real* gold."

Liquor Up Front, Poker in the Rear

POISON PILL

A nice, calm and respectable lady went into the pharmacy, walked up to the pharmacist, looked straight into his eyes, and said, "I would like to buy some cyanide."

The pharmacist asked, "Why in the world do you need cyanide?"

She said, "I need to poison my husband."

The pharmacist's eyes got big and he exclaimed, "Lord have mercy! I can't give you cyanide to kill your husband. That's against the law! I'll lose my license! They'll throw both of us in jail! All kinds of bad things will happen. Absolutely not! You CANNOT have any cyanide!"

The lady reached into her purse and pulled out a picture of her husband in bed with the pharmacist's wife.

The pharmacist looked at the picture and replied, "Well now, that's different. You didn't tell me you had a *prescription!*"

Liquor Up Front, Poker in the Rear

JUNGLE SEX

When Jane first met Tarzan in the jungle she was attracted to him. During her questions about his life, she asked him how he had sex.

"Tarzan not know this sex," he replied.

Jane explained to him what sex was, and Tarzan said, "Oh... Tarzan use knot hole in trunk of tree."

Horrified, Jane said, "Tarzan, you have it all wrong... but I will show you how to do it properly." She took off her clothing and laid down on the ground. "Here," she said, pointing to her pussy, "put it in *here.*"

Tarzan removed his loin cloth, showing Jane his considerable manhood, stepped closer to her, and kicked her in the crotch!

Jane rolled around in agony for what seemed like an eternity. Eventually she managed to grasp for air, and screamed, "What did you do *that* for?"

He replied, "Tarzan check for squirrel."

Liquor Up Front, Poker in the Rear

STRING HIM UP!

On Saturday afternoon I was sitting in my lawn chair, drinking a beer, and watching my wife mow the lawn.

The neighbor lady from across the street was so outraged that she came over and shouted at me, "You should be hung!"

I took a drink from my can of Amstel Lite, wiped the cold foam from my lips, lifted my darkened Ray Ban sunglasses, stared directly into the eyes of this nosy ass neighbor, and then calmly replied, "Actually, I *am*. That's why she cuts the grass!"

Liquor Up Front, Poker in the Rear

A LA CARTE MENU

A crusty old biker out on a long summer ride in the country pulled up to a tavern in the middle of nowhere, parked his bike, and walked inside. As he passed through the swinging doors, he saw a sign hanging over the bar:

COLD BEER: $2.00
HAMBURGER: $2.25
CHEESEBURGER: $2.50
CHICKEN SANDWICH: $3.50
HAND JOB: $50.00

Checking his wallet to be sure he had the necessary payment, the old biker walked up to the bar and beckoned to the exceptionally attractive female bartender who was serving drinks to a couple of sun-wrinkled farmers.

She glided down behind the bar to the old biker. "Yes?" she inquired with a wide, knowing smile, "may I help you?"

Liquor Up Front, Poker in the Rear

The old biker leaned over the bar. "I was wondering young lady," he whispered, "are you the one who gives the hand-jobs?"

She looks into his eyes with that wide smile and purred, "Why yes. Yes, I sure am."

The old biker leaned closer, and into her left ear whispers softly, "Well, wash your hands real good, 'cause I want me a cheeseburger."

Liquor Up Front, Poker in the Rear

SPEAK!

Cowboy: "That your dog?"
Indian: "Yep."
Cowboy: "Mind if I speak to him?"
Indian: "Dog no talk."
Cowboy: "Hey dog, how's it going?"
Dog: "I'm doin' all right."
Indian: (Look of shock!)
Cowboy: "Is this Indian your owner?"
Dog: "Yep."
Cowboy: "How's he treating you?"
Dog: "Real good. He walks me twice a day, feeds me great food and takes me to the lake once a week to play."
Indian: (Look of total disbelief)
Cowboy: "Mind if I talk to your horse?"
Indian: "Horse no talk."
Cowboy: "Hey horse, how's it going?"
Horse: "Cool."
Indian: (Extreme look of shock!)
Cowboy: "Is this your owner?"
Horse: "Yep."

Liquor Up Front, Poker in the Rear

Cowboy: "How's he treating you?"
Horse: "Pretty good. Thanks for asking. He rides me, brushes me often, and keeps me in a lean-to to protect me from the weather."
Indian: (Look of total amazement)
Cowboy: "Mind if I talk to your sheep?"
Indian: "Sheep lie!"

DEAF DOG

My neighbor found out her dog could hardly hear, so she took it to the vet. He found that the problem was hair in its ears, so he cleaned both of them and the dog could hear fine. The vet then proceeded to tell the lady that if she wanted to keep this from re-occurring she should go to the store and get some 'Nair' hair remover and rub it in the dog's ears once a month, so she went to the drug store to get some.

At the register the druggist told her, "If you're going to use this under your arms, don't use deodorant for a few days."

The lady said, "I'm not using it under my arms."

The druggist said, "If you're using it on your legs, don't shave for a couple of days."

"I'm not using it on my legs either. If you must know, I'm using it on my schnauzer."

"I see. In that case, stay off your bicycle for a week!"

Liquor Up Front, Poker in the Rear

THE STOWAWAY

A young, blonde, tipsy woman in Manhattan was so depressed that she decided to end her life by throwing herself into the harbor. She went down to the docks and was about to leap into the water when a handsome young sailor saw her teetering on the edge of the pier, crying.

He took pity on her and said, "Look, you have so much to live for. I'm off to Europe in the morning, and if you like I can stow you away on my ship. I'll take good care of you and bring you food every day." Moving closer, he slipped his arm around her shoulder and added, "I'll keep *you* happy, if you'll keep *me* happy."

The girl nodded yes. After all, what did she have to lose? Perhaps a fresh start in Europe would give her life new meaning.

That night the sailor brought her aboard and hid her in a lifeboat. From then on, every night, he brought her three sandwiches

Liquor Up Front, Poker in the Rear

and a piece of fruit, and they made passionate love until dawn.

Three weeks later, during a routine inspection, she was discovered by the captain. "What are you doing here?" he asked.

"I have an arrangement with one of the sailors," she explained. "I get food and a trip to Europe, and he's screwing me."

"He certainly is," the captain said. "This is the Staten Island Ferry!"

TWO BAGS FULL

A little old lady was walking down the street dragging two large plastic garbage bags behind her. One of the bags ripped, and every once in a while a twenty dollar bill fell out onto the sidewalk.

Noticing this, a policeman stopped her and said, "Ma'am, there are twenty dollar bills falling out of your bag."

"Really? Darn!" said the little old lady. "I'd better go back and see if I can find them. Thanks for telling me officer!"

"Well now, not so fast," said the cop. "How did you get all that money? You didn't steal it, did you?"

"Oh, no," says the little old lady. "You see, my backyard is right next to the football stadium parking lot. On game days a lot of fans come and pee through the fence into my flower garden, so I stand behind the fence with my hedge clippers. Each time some guy sticks his pecker through the fence

Liquor Up Front, Poker in the Rear

I say, 'twenty dollars, or off it comes!'"

"Well, that seems only fair," laughed the cop. "Okay then. Good luck! Oh, by the way, what's in the *other* bag?"

"Well, you know," said the little old lady, "not everybody pays!"

FAMILY TIES

As a woman passed her daughter's closed bedroom door, she heard a strange buzzing noise coming from inside. Opening the door, she observed her daughter masturbating with a vibrator.

Shocked, she asked, "What in the world are you doing?"

The daughter replied, "Mom, I'm thirty-five years old, unmarried, and this thing is about as close as I'll ever get to a husband. Please go away and leave me alone!"

The next day the girl's father heard the same buzzing coming from the other side of the closed bedroom door. Upon entering the room, he observed his daughter making passionate love to her vibrator.

To his query as to what she was doing the daughter rolled her eyes and said, "Dad I'm thirty-five, unmarried, and this thing is about as close as I'll ever get to a husband. Please go away and leave me alone!"

Liquor Up Front, Poker in the Rear

A couple of days later the wife came home from a shopping trip, placed the groceries on the kitchen counter, and heard that buzzing noise coming from, of all places, the living room. She entered the room and saw her husband sitting on the couch downing a cold beer and staring at the television. The vibrator was next to him on the couch, buzzing like crazy.

The wife asked, "What in the hell are you doing?"

The husband replied, "What does it look like? I'm watching football with my son-in-law!"

Liquor Up Front, Poker in the Rear

DING DONG

Upon hearing her elderly grandfather had just passed away, Katie went straight to her grandparent's house to visit her ninety-five-year-old grandmother and comfort her.

When she asked how her grandfather had died her grandmother replied, "He had a heart attack while we were making love on Sunday morning."

Horrified, Katie told her grandmother two people nearly a hundred years old having sex would *surely* be asking for trouble.

"Oh no, my dear," replied granny. "Many years ago, realizing our advanced age, we figured out the best time to do it was when the church bells would start to ring. It was just the right rhythm. Nice and slow and even... nothing too strenuous, simply in on the Ding, and out on the Dong."

She paused to wipe away a tear and continued, "He'd still be alive if the damned ice cream truck hadn't come along!"

Liquor Up Front, Poker in the Rear

HIRED HAND

A successful rancher died and left everything to his devoted wife. She was a very good-looking woman, and determined to keep the ranch, but knew very little about ranching - so she decided to place an ad in the newspaper for a ranch hand.

Two men applied for the job. One was gay, and the other a drunk. She thought long and hard about it, and when no one else applied she decided to hire the gay guy, figuring it would be safer to have him around the house than the drunk.

He proved to be a hard worker who put in long hours every day, and he knew a lot about ranching. For weeks the two of them worked, and the ranch was doing very well.

Then one day the rancher's widow said to the hired hand, "You have done a really good job, and the ranch looks great. You should go into town and kick up your heels."

The hired hand readily agreed, and went

Liquor Up Front, Poker in the Rear

into town one Saturday night.

One o'clock came, and he hadn't returned. Then two o'clock, and still no hired hand. He finally returned around two-thirty, and upon entering the room found the rancher's widow sitting by the fireplace with a glass of wine waiting for him. She waved him over.

The widow looked right at him and said, "Unbutton my blouse and take it off."

Trembling, he did as she directed.

"Now take off my boots."

He did as she asked, ever so slowly.

"Now take off my skirt." He slowly unbuttoned it, constantly watching her eyes in the firelight.

"Now take off my bra."

Again, with trembling hands, he did as he was told and dropped it to the floor.

"And now," she said, "my panties."

By the light of the fire, he slowly pulled them down and off. Then she looked at him and said, "If you *ever* wear my clothes into town again, you're fired!"

Liquor Up Front, Poker in the Rear

THE HOTCAKES

Brenda and Alvin took their six-year-old son to the doctor. With some hesitation they explained that although their little angel appeared to be in good health, they were concerned about his rather small penis.

After carefully examining the child the doctor confidently declared, "Just feed him pancakes. That should solve the problem."

The next morning when the boy arrived at breakfast there was a large stack of warm pancakes in the middle of the table.

"Gee, Mom," he exclaimed. "Are these for me?"

"Just take two," Brenda replied. "The rest are for your father!"

Liquor Up Front, Poker in the Rear

THE NUDIST COLONY

An older man joined a very exclusive nudist colony, and on his first day there he took off his clothes and started to wander around. As he was doing so a gorgeous petite blonde walked by, and the man immediately got an erection.

The woman noticed his erection, came over to him and said, "Did you call for me?"

The man said, "What do you mean?"

She replied, "You must be new here. Let me explain. It's a rule here that if you get an erection, it implies you called for me."

Smiling, she led him to the side of the swimming pool, lay down on a towel, eagerly pulls him to her, and happily let him have his way.

Afterwards the man continued to explore the colony's facilities. He entered the sauna, and as he sat down he farted.

Within moments a huge, hairy man lumbered out of the steam room toward him

Liquor Up Front, Poker in the Rear

saying, "Did you call for me?"

"What do you mean?" said the newcomer.

"You must be new," said the hairy man. "It's a rule that if you fart, it implies you called for me." The huge man then easily spun him around, bent him over a bench, and has his way with him.

The newcomer staggered back to the colony office where he was greeted by the smiling, naked receptionist. "May I help you?" she said.

The man yelled, "Here's my membership card. You can have the key back, and you can keep the five hundred dollar membership fee!"

"But sir, you've only been here for a few hours. You haven't had the chance to see all of our facilities."

The man replied, "Listen lady, I'm sixty-eight years old. I only get an erection once a month, but I fart fifteen times a day! I'm outta here!"

Liquor Up Front, Poker in the Rear

REPEAT OFFENDER

A cop pulled over a brand new red convertible, walked up to the window, and saw a beautiful blonde sitting behind the wheel. He asked for her driver's license, but she didn't know what that was, nor where it was kept… so he told her and she gave it to him.

Then he asked for her registration, and again she had no idea what that was, nor where it was kept… so he told her, and she gave it to him. He then said that he would be right back and he walked back to his car.

The cop got on the radio to tell his friend about the blonde in the red car. His friend told him to give her stuff back, and to pull his pants down. Confused, he walked back to the car, gave her stuff back, and pulled his pants down.

The blonde looked at him, rolled her eyes, and said, "Not *another* breathalizer test!"

CARMEN

A woman scanned the guests at a party, spotted an attractive man standing alone, and approached him.

"My name is Carmen," she told him.

"That's a beautiful name," he replied, "Were you named after someone?"

"No," she replied. "I gave it to myself. It reflects the things I like the most in life - cars, and men."

"So, what's *your* name?" she asked.

He smiled and replied, "B.J. Titsenbeer."

A NEW PLAN

Two married buddies were out drinking one night when one turned to the other and said, "You know, I don't know what else to do. Whenever I go home after we've been out drinking, I turn the headlights off before I get to the driveway. I shut off the engine and coast into the garage. I take my shoes off before I go into the house, sneak up the stairs, and get undressed in the bathroom. I ease carefully into bed, and my wife STILL wakes up and yells at me for staying out so late!"

His buddy looked at him and said, "Well, you're obviously taking the wrong approach. I screech into the driveway, slam the door, storm up the steps, throw my shoes into the closet, jump into bed, rub my hands on my wife's ass and say, 'How about a blowjob?' ... and she's always sound asleep!"

ALL IT TAKES

A Scottish farmer walked into the neighborhood pub and ordered himself a whiskey.

"Ye see that fence over there?" he said to the bartender. "Ah built it with me own two hands! Dug up the holes with me shovel, chopped doon the trees for the posts by me ownself, laid every last rail! But do they call me 'Angus McGregor, the Fence-Builder?' Nooooooo..."

He gulped down the whiskey and ordered another.

"Ye see that pier out on the loch?" he continued. "Ah built it me ownself, too. Swam oot into the loch to lay the foondations, laid doon every single board! But do they call me 'Angus McGregor, the Pier-Builder?' Nooooooo...."

"But ye fuck just ONE sheep ..."

NEXT!

A cowboy from Montana and a cowboy from California were on a sheep drive. They had been out for weeks, and had been pulling sheep out of the mud and working really hard. Eventually they come across a sheep with her head stuck in the fence.

They were both very lonely, so the cowboy from Montana said, "I'm first!" as he dropped his pants and mounted the sheep. When he finished he stepped back, looked at the California cowboy and said, "Okay, you're next!"

So the cowboy from California dropped his pants and stuck his head in the fence.

DAD'S LAMP

One day Little Johnny's teacher, Miss Figpot, asked the class if they could name some things someone can suck.

"An ice cream pop, ma'am!" Little Mary answered.

"Good job Mary," Miss Figpot said. Anyone else?"

"How about a lollipop!" said Steven.

"Very good! Now it's your turn Johnny," the teacher said.

Little Johnny, sitting at back of the room, shouted out, "A lamp!"

The teacher and all of the students wondered about his answer. The teacher then asked him, "Johnny, why do you think one can suck a lamp?"

"Because last night when I passed my parents room I heard my mom say, 'Turn off the lamp honey, and let me suck it!'"

OVERDOSE

There once was a man who just could not keep it going with his wife, so he went to the doctor, who gave him some sex pills. There was a label on the bottle that said:

Take one pill for a great night

It had been a long time since the man had experienced satisfying sex, and he really wanted a *stupendous* night - so he downed the whole bottle.

The following morning the neighbors came over to find the man's son sitting on the porch in tears.

"What's wrong?" they asked.

"I'll tell you what's wrong. Mom's dead, my sister's pregnant, my asshole hurts like hell, and Dad's in the basement yelling, 'Here Kitty, Kitty' ..."

VOICES

A doctor had just finished a marathon sex session with one of his patients. He was resting afterwards, and was feeling a bit guilty because he thought it wasn't really ethical to screw one of his patients.

However a little voice in his head said, "Lots of *other* doctors have sex with their patients... so it's not like you're the first..."

This made the doctor feel a little bit better, until yet another voice in his head said, "But then again... they probably weren't veterinarians..."

Liquor Up Front, Poker in the Rear

SIZING IT UP

Mr. and Mrs. Smith went to a sex therapist who promised to take their case only if he could help them. After hours of tests, he agreed that he could. He told them to stop at the store on the way home and buy some donuts and grapes. Mrs. Smith was to toss the donuts at Mr. Smith's erection, and eat the ones that stayed on. Mr. Smith was to roll the grapes across the floor, and eat the ones that became lodged in Mrs. Smith's vagina. It worked!

A few weeks later the Jones came to see the doctor. "Our friends the Smiths told us to come to you," they said.

The doctor ran the same tests, and told them he was sorry but there was just nothing he could do. The Jones' said, "You helped the Smiths. Why can't you help us?"

After continued begging from the Jones', the doc said "Okay... stop by the market, and buy some Cheerios and a bag of oranges!"

SEX SIGNALS

Two deaf people got married, and during the first week of marriage found they were unable to communicate in the bedroom when the lights were off because neither could see the other using sign language. After several nights of fumbling around and misunderstandings, the wife decided to find a solution.

"Honey," she signed, "Why don't we agree on some simple signals? For instance at night, if you want to have sex with me, reach over and squeeze my *left* breast one time. If you don't want to have sex, reach over and squeeze my *right* breast one time."

The husband thought that was a great idea and signed back to his wife, "Okay. Now, if you want to have sex with me, reach over and pull on my penis *one* time. If you don't want to have sex, reach over and pull on my penis *fifty* times!"

IT WASN'T ME

Bob worked hard, and to keep in shape he spent most evenings bowling or playing basketball at the gym. His wife thought he was pushing himself too hard, so for his birthday she took him to a local strip club.

The doorman at the club greeted them and said, "Hey, Bob! How ya doin'?"

His wife was puzzled, and asked if he had been to that club before.

"Oh no," said Bob. "He's on my bowling team."

Once they were seated a waitress asked Bob if he'd like his usual, and brought over a Budweiser. By now his wife was becoming increasingly uncomfortable so she asked, "How did she know that you drink Budweiser?"

"She's in the Ladies' Bowling League, honey. We share lanes with them."

A stripper then came over to their table, threw her arms around Bob, started to rub

Liquor Up Front, Poker in the Rear

herself all over him, and said, "Hi Bobby. Want your usual table dance, big boy?"

Bob's wife, now furious, grabbed her purse and stormed out of the club. Bob followed, and spotted her getting into a cab. Before she could slam the door he jumped in beside her and tried desperately to explain how the stripper must have mistaken him for someone else - but his wife was having none of it.

She screamed at him at the top of her lungs, calling him every four letter word in the book. Finally the cabby turned around and said, "Geez Bob, you sure picked up a real bitch *this* time!"

Liquor Up Front, Poker in the Rear

QUID PRO QUO

There was a couple who had been married for twenty years, and every time they made love the husband always insisted on shutting off the light.

Well, after twenty years the wife felt it was getting ridiculous. She decided to break him out of this crazy habit so one night, while they were in the middle of a wild, screaming, romantic session, she turned on the lights.

She looked down, and saw that her husband was holding a dildo in his hand! It was soft, wonderful, and larger than a real one.

She went completely ballistic. "You impotent bastard," she screamed at him. "How could you keep lying to me all of these years? You'd better explain yourself!"

The husband looked her straight in the eyes and says calmly, "Okay... I'll explain the toy... and *you* explain the kids!"

Liquor Up Front, Poker in the Rear

BANG!

A man was having issues with premature ejaculation, so he decided to go to the doctor to see what could be done to cure him.

The doctor said, "When you feel like you are getting ready to ejaculate, try startling yourself."

That very same day the man went to the store and bought himself a starter pistol. All excited to try out the suggestion, he ran home to his wife.

At home his wife was in bed, naked and waiting. As the two began they found themselves in the '69' position and the man, moments later, felt the sudden urge to come – so he fired the starter pistol.

The next day the doctor asked the man, "So, how did it go?"

"Not that well... when I fired the pistol my wife shit on my face, bit three inches off my penis, and my neighbor came out of the closet with his hands in the air!"

PERSONAL AD

A lonely woman in her seventies decided that it was time to get married again, so she put an ad in the local paper that read:

HUSBAND WANTED!
MUST BE IN MY AGE GROUP (70's),
MUST NOT BEAT ME,
MUST NOT RUN AROUND ON ME,
AND MUST STILL BE GOOD IN BED!
PLEASE APPLY IN PERSON.

On the second day she heard the doorbell. Much to her dismay, she opened the door to see a gray-haired gentleman with no arms or legs sitting in a wheelchair. The old woman said, "You're not really asking me to consider you, are you? Just look at you... you have no legs!"

The old man smiled, "Therefore I cannot run around on you!"

She snorted. "You don't have any hands

Liquor Up Front, Poker in the Rear

either!"

Again the old man smiled, "That's right, and therefore I can never beat you!"

She raised an eyebrow and gazed intently. "Hmmm... are you still good in bed?"

With that the old gentleman leaned back, beamed a big broad smile and said, "I rang the doorbell, didn't I?"

Liquor Up Front, Poker in the Rear

FEMALE PHARMACY

A man went into a pharmacy and asked to speak with a male pharmacist. The woman who was behind the counter said that she was the pharmacist, that she and her sister owned the store, and that there were no males employed there. She then asked if there was something she could help the gentleman with.

The man said it was something he would be much more comfortable discussing with a male pharmacist.

The female pharmacist assured him that she was a professional and whatever it was that he needed to discuss, he could be confident that she would treat him with the highest level of professionalism.

The man agreed and began by saying, "This is tough for me to discuss, but I have a permanent erection. All day... all night... it never goes away! It causes me a lot of problems, and severe embarrassment. So I was wondering… what you can give me for it?"

The pharmacist said, "Just a minute, I have to go speak with my sister."

When she returned she said, "We discussed it at length, and the absolute best we can do is one third ownership in the store, a company car, and three thousand dollars a month for living expenses…"

Liquor Up Front, Poker in the Rear

NUMBER FOUR

A couple had just gotten married, and on the night of their honeymoon, before making passionate love, the wife told her husband, "Please be gentile, I'm still a virgin."

The shocked husband replied, "How is this possible? You've been married three times before!"

The wife responded, "Well, my *first* husband was a gynecologist, and all he wanted to do was look at it. My *second* husband was a psychiatrist, and all he wanted to do was talk about it. Finally, my *third* husband was a stamp collector, and all he wanted to do was... *oh*... I sure do miss him!"

A SMALL PROBLEM

Two friends who happened to be dwarfs decided to treat themselves to a vacation in Las Vegas. Drunk and at the hotel bar, they were dazzled by two women and wound up taking them to their separate hotel rooms.

The first dwarf and his woman tried everything they could, but he was just too drunk to get an erection. To make matters worse, he heard cries of "ONE, TWO, THREE… HUGHHHHHHHHH!" all night long from the next room where his friend and the other woman were.

In the morning the second dwarf asked the first, "How did it go?"

The first whispered back, "It was so embarrassing. I simply couldn't get an erection!"

The second dwarf shook his head, "You think *that's* embarrassing? I couldn't even get on the bed!"

BECAUSE HE CAN'T

Two drunks had just gotten thrown out of a bar and were walking down the street when they came across a stray dog sitting on the curb, licking his balls. They stood there watching, and after a while one of them said, "I sure wish I could do that!"

The other one looked at him and said, "Well, if I were you, I think I'd *pet* him a little bit first!"

GOOD JOB

A man and his wife went back to their honeymoon hotel for their twenty-fifth wedding anniversary and got the very same room as before. As the couple reflected on that magical evening twenty-five years ago the wife asked the husband, "When you first saw my naked body in front of you, what was going through your mind?"

The husband replied, "Well, all I wanted to do was to fuck your brains out, and suck your tits dry."

Then, as the wife undressed, she asked, "So... what are you thinking now?"

He replied, "I'm thinking I did a damn good job!"

WEDDED BLISS

A man and a woman who had never met before found themselves in the same sleeping carriage of a train. After the initial embarrassment they both went to sleep, with the man on the top bunk and the woman on the lower.

In the middle of the night the man leaned over, woke up the woman and said, "I'm sorry to bother you, but I'm awfully cold... and was wondering if you could possibly get me another blanket?"

The woman leaned out and with a glint in her eye said, "I have a better idea. Just for tonight, let's pretend that we're married!"

The man couldn't believe his good fortune and said happily, "Sure... that sounds great!"

The woman then said, "Good... go get your own fucking blanket!"

Liquor Up Front, Poker in the Rear

REMINISCING

There were three generations of prostitutes living together - a mother, a daughter and a grandmother. One night the daughter came home looking very down.

"How did you do tonight dear?" asked her mother.

"Not too good..." replied the daughter, "I only got twenty dollars for a blow job."

"Wow!" said the mother. "In *my* day we gave a blow job for fifty cents!"

"Good God!" said the Grandmother, "In *my* day we were just glad to get something warm in our stomachs!"

PLAN B

A man woke up out of a deep sleep and, feeling really horny, nudged his wife awake and asked, "Why don't we get it on baby?"

She replied, "I have an appointment at the gynecologist tomorrow, and you know I don't like to make love the night before."

The husband reluctantly agreed, rolled over, and started to go back to sleep.

A few minutes later he nudged his wife again and asked, "You don't by any chance have a *dentist's* appointment tomorrow, do you?"

Liquor Up Front, Poker in the Rear

DON'T ASK DON'T TELL

A beautiful woman walked into a doctor's office, and the doctor was bowled over by how stunningly awesome she was... and all of his professionalism went right out the window.

He told her to take off her pants, and once she had complied he began rubbing her thighs. "Do you know what I am doing?" asks the doctor.

She replied, "Yes, you are checking for abnormalities."

He then told her to take off her shirt and bra, and she did. The doctor began rubbing her breasts and asked, "Do you know what I am doing now?"

"Yes, checking for cancer."

Finally he told her to take off her panties, laid her down on the table, got on top, and started having sex with her. He asked, "Do you know what I am doing now?"

She replied, "Yes, getting herpes – that's why I'm here!"

FUCKED AGAIN

A police officer was patrolling the highway when he saw a naked man tied to a tree, crying. The officer stopped and approached the guy.

"What's going on here?" he asked.

The guy sobbed, "I was driving along, and picked up a hitchhiker. He pulled a gun on me, robbed me, took all my money, my clothes, my car, and then tied me up to this tree and then left."

The cop studied the guy for a moment, pulled down his pants, and whipped out his dick. "Well, I guess just this just isn't your lucky day, pal…"

Liquor Up Front, Poker in the Rear

GO FOR THE GOLD

A man was out shopping and discovered a new brand of prophylactics called 'Olympic Condoms.' Clearly impressed, he bought a pack. Upon getting home he told his wife about the purchase he had just made.

"*Olympic* condoms?" she blurted, "What makes them so special?"

"There are three colors," he replied, "Gold, Silver, and Bronze."

"What color are you going to wear tonight?" she asked cheekily.

"Gold, of course," said the man proudly.

The wife responded, "Why don't you wear Silver? It would be nice if you came *second* for a change!"

FAR AWAY

A trucker entered a whorehouse, handed the Madam eight hundred dollars in cash, and said, "I want your ugliest woman, and a crappy bologna sandwich on stale bread."

The astonished Madam replied, "For *that* kind of money you could have one of my finest girls and a gourmet dinner."

The trucker said, "I know, but I'm not horny or hungry… just homesick!"

Liquor Up Front, Poker in the Rear

CUT THE SCHLITZ

A man walked into a bar and asked the bartender for a case of beer, and specified he wanted any kind except Schlitz.

The bartender said, "What's wrong with Schlitz? Don't you like it?"

The man says, "I *hate* that shit. Last night I drank a whole case of Schlitz, and ended up blowing chunks."

The bartender said, "Buddy, if you drink a whole case of *any* beer you're going to blow chunks."

"You don't understand," said the man, "Chunks is the name of my dog!"

Liquor Up Front, Poker in the Rear

GONE FISHING

One Saturday morning I got up early, put on my long johns, dressed quietly, made my lunch, grabbed the dog, slipped into the garage to hook the boat up to the truck, and proceeded to back out into a torrential downpour.

There was snow mixed with the rain and the wind was blowing at fifty miles per hour, so I pulled back into the garage, turned on the radio, and discovered that the weather would be bad throughout the day.

Disappointed, I went back into the house, quietly undressed, and slipped back into bed. There I cuddled up to my wife's back, now with a different anticipation, and whispered, "The weather out there is *terrible.*"

She sleepily replied, "It sure is... can you believe that stupid husband of mine is out fishing in that shit?"

Liquor Up Front, Poker in the Rear

BAD KARMA

A successful businessman flew to Vegas for the weekend to gamble. He lost the shirt off his back, and had nothing left but a quarter and the second half of his round-trip ticket. If he could just get to the airport he could get himself home, so he went out to the front of the casino where there was a cab waiting, got in, and explained his situation to the cabby. He promised to send the driver money from home, he offered him his credit card numbers, his driver's license number, his address, etc. all to no avail.

The cabby said, "If you don't have fifteen dollars, get the hell out of my cab!" So the businessman was forced to hitch-hike to the airport and was barely in time for his flight.

One year later the businessman, having worked long and hard to regain his financial success, returned to Vegas and this time he won big. Feeling pretty good about himself, he went out to the front of the casino to get a cab ride back to the airport, and who should

Liquor Up Front, Poker in the Rear

he see out there at the end of a long line of cabs but his old buddy who had refused him a ride when he was down on his luck. The businessman thought for a moment about how he could make the guy pay for his lack of charity, and hit on a plan.

The businessman got in the first cab in line and asked, "How much for a ride to the airport?"

"Fifteen bucks," came the reply.

"And how much for you to give me a blow job on the way?"

"What? Get the hell out of my cab!"

The businessman then got into the back of each cab in line and asked the very same questions, with the same result. When he got to his old friend at the back of the line he got in and asked, "How much for a ride to the airport?"

The cabby replied, "fifteen bucks."

The businessman said, "Okay!" and off they went.

Then, as they drove slowly past the long line of cabs, the businessman gave a smile and thumbs up sign to each and every driver.

Liquor Up Front, Poker in the Rear

AT THE MARKET

Sue and Jane were shopping together at the supermarket, and when they got to the vegetable section Jane picked up a big cucumber and commented about how it reminded her of her husband's penis.

Sue said, "Wow!" and not to be outdone hefted a good sized potato in each hand while saying, "You know Jane, these remind me of *my* husband's *balls.*"

Impressed, Jane said, "Hmm, they're that big, huh?"

"No," Sue answered. "That dirty!"

Liquor Up Front, Poker in the Rear

THE NEW MAID

A man dialed his home phone from work, and a strange woman answered. The man said, "Who is this?"

"This is the maid," responded the woman.

"What? We don't have a maid!"

"I was just hired this morning by the lady of the house."

"Well, this is her husband. Is she there?"

"Ummm.... she's upstairs in the bedroom having sex with someone... who I just figured was her husband!"

"How do you know that's what they're doing?"

"Well sir, the bedsprings are creaking like crazy, the headboard has been banging against the wall for the past hour, and she has screamed 'I'm coming!' at least six times..."

The man was fuming! He said to the maid, "Listen, would you like to make fifty thousand dollars?"

"What do I have to do?"

Liquor Up Front, Poker in the Rear

"Get my gun from my desk in the den and shoot that witch... and the jerk she is with too!"

The maid put down the phone, and the man heard footsteps... followed by two gunshots.

The maid came back to the phone and said, "Okay, I did it. What should I do with the bodies?"

"Throw them in the swimming pool!"

"What? There's no pool here sir!"

Then, after a long pause... "Uh.... is this 555-1811?"

Liquor Up Front, Poker in the Rear

DEAD WOOD

A man died while making love to his wife, and a few days later the undertaker called her and said, "Your husband still has a hard-on. What shall I do with it?"

The wife replied, "Cut it off, and shove it up his ass!"

The undertaker did as he was told.

On the day of the funeral the wife visited her husband for the last time and saw a tear rolling down his face, so she whispered in his ear, "It fucking hurts, doesn't it!"

ON VACATION

Three men went on vacation abroad together, and the tourist office informed them that there was only one hotel in town with any vacancies.

They went straight there, only to be told by the desk clerk that there is only one room available in the entire hotel.

They weren't too keen about the idea, but since it was their only option they took the room for one evening and shared its one and only bed.

Surprisingly, that night they all enjoyed a good night's sleep. In the morning the man on the right side of the bed said, "I dreamt I had the best sex last night!"

The guy on the left side said, "That's funny, I had the exact same dream!"

The guy in the middle said, "Not me. I dreamt I was skiing…"

Liquor Up Front, Poker in the Rear

CHINESE DOCTOR

A woman was very distraught by the fact that she had not had a date or any sex in quite some time. She was afraid she might have something wrong with her, so she decided to seek the medical expertise of a sex therapist. Her doctor recommended that she see a very well known Chinese sex therapist by the name of Dr. Chang.

She went to see him, and upon entering the examination room Dr. Chang said "Okay, take off all your crose."

The woman did as she was told.

"Now get down on the floor and craw reery, reery fass to odderside of room."

Once again the woman did as she was instructed.

Dr. Chang then said "Okay, now craw reery, reery fass back to me."

So she did.

Dr. Chang shook his head slowly and said "Your probrem vewy bad. You haf Ed Zachary diease. Worse case I ever see. Dat

Liquor Up Front, Poker in the Rear

why you not haf sex or dates."

Worried, the woman asked anxiously, "Oh my God, Dr. Chang! What in the world is Ed Zachary Disease?"

Dr. Chang sighed deeply and replied, "Ed Zachary Disease is condition when your face look Ed Zachary like your ass..."

ALL OVER TAN

There was once a man who really took care of his body and jogged six miles every day. One morning he looked into the mirror, and while admiring his body noticed that he was suntanned all over with the exception of his penis – so he decided to do something about it.

He went to the beach, stripped, and buried himself in the sand – all except for his penis, which he left sticking out. A short time later two little old ladies came strolling along the beach.

On seeing the thing sticking out of the sand, one of them began to move it around with her cane, and remarked to the other little old lady, "There is no justice in the world!"

The other little old lady said, "What do you mean by that, Mildred?"

The first little old lady said, "Look at that! When I was twenty... I was curious about them. When I was thirty... I enjoyed them.

Liquor Up Front, Poker in the Rear

When I was forty... I asked for them. When I was fifty... I paid for them. When I was sixty... I prayed for them. When I was seventy... I forgot about them. And now that I am eighty, the damned things are growing wild, and I'm too old to squat!"

Liquor Up Front, Poker in the Rear

JUST RELAX

An escaped convict, imprisoned for first degree murder, had spent twenty-five years of his life sentence in prison. While on the run, he broke into a house and tied up a young couple who had been sleeping in their bedroom.

He tied the man to a chair on one side of the room, and his wife onto the bed on the other side of the room. The convict got on the bed, and it appeared to the husband that he may have been kissing his wife's neck. Suddenly, the convict got up and left the room.

Seizing the opportunity, the husband made his way across the room with the chair in tow and leaned over his pretty young wife, who was bound up on the bed in a skimpy nightgown. He whispered, "Honey, this guy hasn't seen a woman in years. I saw him kissing on your neck right before he left. Just relax. Cooperate with anything he wants. If he wants to have sex with you, just

Liquor Up Front, Poker in the Rear

go along with it and pretend that you like it. Whatever you do, don't fight him or make him mad. Our lives depend on it!"

"Honey," the wife said, spitting out her gag, "I'm so relieved you feel that way. You're right, he *hasn't* seen a woman in years... but he wasn't kissing my neck. He was whispering in my ear. He told me he thinks you're really cute, and asked where we keep the Vaseline..."

KISS OF LIFE

A woman was in a coma, and the nurses were in her room giving her a sponge bath. One of them was washing her 'private area,' and noticed there was a response on the monitor when she touched her there.

They went to her husband and explained what had happened, telling him, "Crazy as this may sound, maybe a little oral sex will do the trick and bring her out of the coma."

The husband was skeptical, but they assured him that they would close the curtains for privacy. It was worth a try, so hubby finally agreed and went into his wife's room.

After a few minutes the woman's monitor flat-lined... there was no pulse... and no heartbeat! The nurses ran into the room and found the husband standing there pulling up his trousers while saying, "Everything was fine at *first,* but then she started to choke…"

Liquor Up Front, Poker in the Rear

PROUD PAPA

A teenage boy came home with a big smile on his face, and his mom asked, "What did you do at school today honey?"

"Oh, I had sex with my teacher," he said calmly.

The mother began to scream and yell and sent him to his room until his father got home.

When the father arrived the mother said in tears, "Go talk to your son... he had sex with his teacher today!"

The dad walked upstairs with a big grin on his face. He asked what had happened at school, and the son told him.

The dad said, "Son I'm so proud of you! I'm going to get you that bike you have always wanted."

So they went out and bought the bike, and the dad asked the son if he wanted to ride it when they got home.

The boy replied, "Not today dad. My ass is still sore!"

GOING POSTAL

It was near Christmas, and a mailman was out delivering packages on his route when a beautiful blonde woman opened her front door wearing a sexy negligee and invited him inside. Surprised, he followed her to the bedroom where they proceeded to have sex. After they were finished the woman got dressed and handed the man a dollar.

The puzzled mailman asked, "Why are you giving me a dollar?"

The woman replied, "Well, when I was making my shopping list I asked my husband what should we give the nice mailman for Christmas and he said, "Fuck the mailman, give him a dollar!"

Liquor Up Front, Poker in the Rear

MONEY TALKS

Larry got home late one night and his wife said, "Where in the hell have you been?"

Larry replied, "I was out getting a tattoo."

"A tattoo?" she frowned. "What kind did you get?"

"'I got a hundred dollar bill on my penis!" he said proudly.

"What the hell were you thinking?" She said, shaking her head in disgust. "Why on earth would an accountant get a hundred dollar bill tattooed on his penis?"

"Well, for one thing, I like to watch my money grow. Two, every once in a while I like to play with my money. Three, I like how money feels in my hand… and lastly, instead of you going out shopping, you can stay right here at home and blow a hundred bucks anytime you want!"

Liquor Up Front, Poker in the Rear

IT'S YOUR CHOICE

One bright and sunny morning a husband turned to his lovely wife and said, "Wife, we're going fishing this weekend - you, me and the dog."

The wife grimaced, "But I don't *like* fishing!"

"Look! We're going fishing and that's final."

"Do I have to go? I really don't want to!"

"Okay, I'll give you three choices... one, you come fishing with me and the dog... two, you give me a blowjob, or three, you take it up the ass!"

The wife grimaced. "But I don't want to do *any* of those things!"

"Wife, I've given you three options... you'll have to choose one of them! I'm going to the garage to sort out my fishing tackle, when I come back I expect you to have made up your mind!"

The wife sat and thought about it, and

Liquor Up Front, Poker in the Rear

twenty minutes later her husband came back.

"Well! What have you decided? Fishing with me and the dog, a blowjob, or up the ass?"

The wife complained some more, and then finally made up her mind. "Okay, I'll give you a blow job!"

"Great!" he said as he dropped his pants.

The wife got on her knees and began doing her business, but suddenly stopped and looked up at her husband. "Oh! It tastes absolutely disgusting... it tastes all shitty!"

"Yeah," said her husband, "the dog didn't want to go fishing either!"

Liquor Up Front, Poker in the Rear

www.ingramcontent.com/pod-product-compliance
Lightning Source LLC
Chambersburg PA
CBHW061637040426
42446CB00010B/1454